Once Upon A Brand

Once Upon A Brand

The Business of Storytelling

Jon Smith

BAL
KON
media

ONCE UPON A BRAND:
THE BUSINESS OF STORYTELLING

Published by Balkon Media

Paperback edition ISBN: 978-1-916970-07-6
Hardcover edition ISBN: 978-1-916970-08-3
Also available in e-book format

www.balkon.media

For Uncle Joey —
The greatest storyteller this side
of the Ballinamore-Ballyconnell Canal.

Much loved, much missed.

Also by Jon Smith

The Power of Storytelling in Business

Welcome to *Once Upon a Brand: The Business of Storytelling*.

Imagine a sea of content—blogs, emails, social posts—all vying for attention yet fading into a blur, forgotten moments after they're read. It's an ocean most brands are drowning in, despite their best efforts. You're likely familiar with the process: you craft the perfect post, check the SEO, fine-tune the benefits list, and click *publish*, only to find that your meticulously created content has barely made a ripple.

But why? Why does it feel like your brand's message is echoing into a void? The answer is deceptively simple: your audience doesn't remember facts; they remember stories. Stories that connect, inspire, and resonate are the ones that cut through the noise, turning disengaged skimmers into loyal fans and passive readers into active participants.

Think back to the last piece of content that truly caught your attention. Was it a generic list of features or a narrative that made you feel something, even if just for a moment? That's the power of storytelling. It's the unquantifiable magic that transforms a pitch into a movement, a product into a trusted companion, and a brand into a household name.

Storytelling isn't new; it's ancient. Long before marketing strategies and click-through rates, stories moved people. They sparked revolutions, built communities, and defined legacies. Stories are how we connect, remember, and take action. And in today's hyper-competitive world, storytelling is what will set your brand apart from the masses.

Once Upon a Brand isn't just about why storytelling works; it's about how you can weave it into the fabric of your business, from the boardroom to the blog post. Founders will find ways to infuse their vision with heart, making investors lean in. Marketers will see how campaigns that start with stories become the ones people talk about. Sales teams will discover how stories not only sell but stick. And product leaders will learn how to turn dry feature launches into compelling narratives that draw users in.

So, why should you care? Because brands that fail to master storytelling risk being ignored. The digital landscape is crowded, and simply shouting louder won't help. Stories, however, will.

This is your chance to change how your brand is perceived, engaged with, and remembered. *Once Upon a Brand: The Business of Storytelling* will show you how to make your brand's story one that people remember and repeat—leading to your very own *happily ever after*.

Part One

THE ART OF

STORYTELLING

Chapter 1
What Makes a Good Story? – Elements and Structure

So, what really makes a good story? You might think it's all about a snappy beginning or an epic twist at the end. While those can help, they're not enough. A good story is more than just a punchy tagline or a quirky plot. It's a journey—one that hooks your audience from the start and keeps them invested all the way through to the payoff.

Let's not kid ourselves: people don't have time for weak stories. Your audience is bombarded with content daily, much of it about as engaging as watching paint dry. To stand out, your story must do three things: grab attention, sustain interest, and evoke a response. Whether you're writing an ad, crafting a pitch, or launching a social media campaign, these principles remain the same. So, let's break down the elements that make a story worth hearing (or, in this case, reading).

The Hook: An Opening That Demands Attention

Picture this: you're at a party. The room is filled with chatter, and someone starts a story with, "So, I was in the supermarket the other day..." You tune out, right? Compare that to: "I found a lottery ticket on the floor, and what happened next was insane." Boom—you're hooked. In storytelling, the hook is the promise of something that compels your audience to stay. It's the opening line that makes them put down their phone, stop scrolling, or lean in closer.

The same rule applies to your brand's content. If your story starts with "Our company is proud to offer...," congratulations—you've lost them. Try something bolder, something that invites curiosity. "We thought we were launching just another product, until it saved a life." See the difference? Your hook should make people think, "I need to know more."

The Core: Building Tension and Interest

The best stories don't just dangle a hook and fizzle out. They sustain interest by adding layers. Think of the tension in a good novel or a gripping movie—there's always a sense that something is building. In brand storytelling, the core of your narrative is where you show transformation, conflict, or a journey.

This isn't about padding your story with fluff. Every word counts. Whether it's the struggle of a start-up that beat the odds, a customer who found unexpected value in your product, or a bold company pivot, make sure there's progression. Audiences are drawn to growth and change. It's the *how* that keeps them reading and engaged.

And here's a tip: don't be afraid to show vulnerability. Some of the most powerful brand stories don't revolve around perfect products or flawless leaders. They show the messy middle, the risk, the almost-failures, and the lessons learned. Why? Because it's relatable. People love seeing that brands are human too.

The Payoff: Ending with Impact—If you've ever read a book or watched a film that ended without any closure, you know how frustrating it is. Your brand's story needs an ending that justifies the time your audience has spent with it. This is where you deliver on the promise you made in the hook. It's the reveal, the resolution, the "aha" moment.

In marketing terms, your payoff could be an inspiring outcome, a surprising benefit of your service, or an emotional twist that connects your audience on a deeper level. But here's the key: don't oversell and underdeliver. A payoff should feel earned, leaving the audience with a sense of satisfaction, insight, or even a desire to act.

The Structure: The Classic Frameworks

Great stories don't happen by accident. Even the best storytellers follow structures that guide their narratives. The most well-known? The three-act structure: the beginning (setup), middle (conflict), and end (resolution). This model works across all mediums, including your brand's storytelling. It gives you a natural flow—hook your audience, take them on a journey, and land them with a conclusion that resonates.

Consider another famous structure: the Hero's Journey. You know it from movies like *Star Wars* and *The Lord of the Rings*—an ordinary character ventures out, faces challenges, and returns changed. Apply this to your brand by positioning your customers as the hero and your product or service as the guide. It's their story, not yours, and you're there to help them succeed. We will look at this in greater detail in Chapter Four.

Your Story, Their Attention

Remember, the elements of a good story don't just create interest; they build trust. Stories that resonate remind your audience that your brand is more than just a company—it's an experience, an ally, even a source of inspiration.

So, as we move deeper into the world of business storytelling, keep these questions in mind: Does your story have a strong hook? Does it build genuine interest? And does it end with impact? Nail these, and you won't just have content—you'll have stories people remember, share, and act on.

To transform your brand's content from *must-ignore* to *must-read* we shall look at examples from Subscriba, a (fictitious) SaaS subscription management platform. In this case, the 'About Us' page on their website.

Subscriba - About Us

Subscriba is a SaaS subscription management platform that helps businesses track, manage, and optimise their technology spending. Our platform offers features like subscription tracking, cost monitoring, automated renewal reminders, user utilisation insights, contract management, and spend forecasting.

Subscriba is designed for CFOs, finance teams, IT managers, and procurement departments in mid-to-large-sized businesses across various sectors, including tech, e-commerce, financial services, and healthcare. Our goal is to provide businesses with visibility into their SaaS ecosystem to reduce costs, eliminate waste, and improve ROI on software investments.

With integrations to major SaaS providers such as Salesforce, Slack, Microsoft 365, and others, Subscriba centralises all subscription data, allowing organisations to monitor usage and receive alerts for renewals, cost spikes, and underutilised licenses. By leveraging our comprehensive dashboard, companies can streamline their technology management and make informed decisions.

This is a pretty standard 'About Us' page for a SaaS business. Maybe it resembles yours? In fairness, it provides all the basic facts about Subscriba, but it reads like a list of features and benefits without any emotional connection or compelling reason for the reader to care. It's informative but lacks a hook and doesn't draw the reader into a story. In simple terms it leaves the reader thinking, *Yeah? And?* Now let's look at the same About Us page with some storytelling elements baked in:

Subscriba - About Us

Imagine you're the CFO of a fast-growing company. Your teams are thriving, productivity is up, but your SaaS subscriptions are a tangled web of costs, contracts, and overlapping services. It's easy to lose sight of what's essential and what's bleeding your budget dry. That's where Subscriba steps in.

At Subscriba, we understand the chaos of managing multiple SaaS tools across departments. We've built a powerful platform that goes beyond basic tracking to become your partner in subscription optimisation. Our comprehensive dashboard pulls together all your subscription data—costs, contract terms, renewal dates, user utilisation—into one intuitive, centralised view.

With real-time integration to top SaaS platforms like Salesforce, Microsoft 365, and Google Workspace, Subscriba keeps your tech stack transparent and manageable. We're here to help CFOs, finance teams, IT managers, and procurement departments regain control, prevent surprises, and cut out waste. Our automated renewal reminders ensure you never miss a renegotiation opportunity, while user insights help you scale smartly, not blindly.

In a world where every dollar counts, Subscriba is the edge that keeps your business agile, efficient, and always a step ahead.

This version immediately puts the reader in a relatable scenario, creating an emotional connection with the audience by presenting a challenge they understand and may actually be experiencing right now.

The introduction acts as a hook, drawing the reader in with an engaging scenario. The core builds on this by highlighting Subscriba's features as solutions to real pain points, not just as generic tools. Finally, the payoff is clear: a promise that Subscriba makes managing SaaS subscriptions not just possible, but strategic and advantageous.

This storytelling approach makes the content memorable and relatable, ensuring readers feel understood and see Subscriba as an essential partner in their success.

Does your About Us page capture attention, build interest, and leave a lasting impression? Or does it fizzle out before it even begins? If it's missing a strong hook, core, or payoff, it's time to fix it. Start today and make your stories worth remembering.

Chapter 2
The Psychology Behind Storytelling – Why Stories Work

Let's start with a truth that marketers and business owners often forget: humans are wired for stories. We crave them, respond to them, and most importantly, we remember them. Facts and data? Sure, they have their place, but they're often forgotten faster than yesterday's lunch. *Increase your revenue, provides cost savings, helps maximise profits...* they're just random words that don't mean anything and are quickly forgotten. Stories, on the other hand, stick with us. Why? Because storytelling is an evolutionary superpower. To understand why stories work, we need to look at how they tap into the human mind.

Stories Are Built for the Brain

Think about the last time you heard a compelling story. Your mind didn't just hear the words; it *saw* the scene unfold, felt the emotions, and maybe even anticipated what would come next. This isn't by accident. Our brains are wired to process stories as complete experiences. When we hear facts and figures alone, the language processing parts of our brains light up—useful, but not engaging. But when we hear a story, *multiple* areas of the brain come alive, including those responsible for sensory experiences and emotions. It's as if we're living the story ourselves.

This is why a story about Subscriba saving a company from thousands in lost SaaS costs will resonate more than just stating, "Subscriba optimises SaaS spend." The latter is forgettable; the former? Memorable, applicable and compelling.

Emotional Engagement: The Glue That Binds

If you think business is purely rational, think again. Studies show that emotions drive decisions. In fact, emotions have been shown to be the primary factor in making purchase decisions, with logic coming in as a backup to justify the choice after the fact. So, when your content hits the emotional sweet spot, you're not just engaging your audience —you're winning them over.

Storytelling excels because it naturally weaves emotion into facts. Consider this: when telling your brand's story, you could rattle off statistics about cost savings, user retention, and increased ROI. Or, you could share the story of an IT manager who, thanks to Subscriba's timely renewal alerts, saved their company from a six-figure auto-renewal nightmare. Which would you remember? Which would you share? Which would you act upon?

The Power of Mirror Neurons

Here's where things get really fascinating. Our brains have something called mirror neurons, which are activated when we watch someone else's actions or emotions. It's why we flinch when we see someone about to take a fall, or feel a thrill when the underdog wins in a movie. Stories harness this power by allowing your audience to experience your brand's journey as if it were their own.

So, when Subscriba (a fictitious brand referred to throughout this book) shares a customer story of a CFO who turned their company's

SaaS chaos into streamlined efficiency, the audience isn't just reading —they're *feeling* the stress of out-of-control spending, followed by the relief of finding a solution. This shared emotional journey builds empathy and trust, turning your audience from passive readers into engaged believers.

How Stories Build Trust and Credibility

People don't trust brands; they trust people. Brands that leverage stories show their human side, becoming relatable and approachable. By sharing narratives that showcase vulnerability, challenges, and triumphs, brands can break down the cold corporate wall and invite audiences in. A story about a rough patch your company overcame, a risky pivot that paid off, or even a customer's struggle turned success doesn't just showcase your brand's strength; it shows your authenticity.

In a market filled with jargon-laden, impersonal content, stories stand out because they're real. They're relatable. When Subscriba talks about the problem of SaaS sprawl and how it's helped companies regain control, it's not just promoting a product; it's demonstrating an understanding of the reader's daily struggles and positioning itself as a trustworthy partner.

The Storytelling Formula in Action

Let's break down the typical structure of how stories work on the mind. First, there's the hook—an opening that seizes attention and promises something intriguing. This is followed by the core, or in movie parlance the second act, which builds interest by adding layers, context, or conflict. Finally, there's the payoff—the resolution or insight that leaves the audience with a sense of satisfaction or a call to action.

This three-act structure isn't just a writer's trick; it's the way our brains are programmed to digest information. The pattern feels natural and fulfilling. When brands use this structure, they align their content with the way audiences are already primed to engage, making it more impactful and memorable.

Why This Matters for Your Brand

You might be thinking, "Okay, so stories are powerful. But how does this help my brand?" Here's the thing: storytelling isn't just about creating a narrative; it's about strategically embedding it into your brand's DNA. When Subscriba tells stories about how it empowered CFOs to regain control over their tech budget, it's doing more than sharing a win—it's illustrating that Subscriba understands, cares, and delivers.

A brand that tells stories is a brand that people remember, relate to, and trust. And trust? That's the cornerstone of any successful business relationship.

So, as we move forward, keep this in mind: facts inform, but stories transform. They transform your audience's perception, your brand's image, and, ultimately, your bottom line. Ready to create stories that stick? Let's dive deeper by looking at an example of an Our Customers web page.

Most tech companies showcase some of their customers. Whether its customer logos in a slider about three quarters of the way down on the homepage, or a dedicated 'Our Customers' page, brands do it for social proof—don't just take our word for it, look at some of these (hopefully) household names who spend money with us, you should too...

Done right, it's a powerful persuader for prospects, especially for newer companies trying to build up their brand equity. But most brands don't do it right, they do it boring.

Here's an example 'Our customers' page:

Our customers
Subscriba is trusted by mid-to-large businesses across various sectors, including technology, e-commerce, financial services, and healthcare. Our platform is designed to meet the needs of CFOs, IT managers, and procurement departments who need comprehensive SaaS subscription management solutions.

From tracking and managing subscription costs to optimising user utilisation and preventing unnecessary auto-renewals, our customers rely on Subscriba to provide full visibility into their technology spend. Businesses across APAC, LATAM, and ME regions have chosen Subscriba for our robust integration capabilities, actionable insights, and cost-saving features.

Join the many companies that have improved their ROI, streamlined their subscription management, and regained control over their SaaS ecosystem with Subscriba.

The page lists general information about Subscriba's clientele and the platform's benefits. It's factual and provides a broad overview, but it lacks the personal connection and emotional engagement that build trust and relatability. The language is formal and informative, but it doesn't inspire or invite the reader to see themselves in the narrative. I've read hundreds of similar pages, and I'm sure you have too. Look what happens when we employ elements of good storytelling:

Our customers: Real Stories, Real Success
Imagine being an IT manager overwhelmed by dozens of SaaS subscriptions, each with its own renewal schedule and user list. Or a CFO trying to get a clear view of how much each department is spending on software, only to find that key details are scattered across countless spreadsheets. This is where Subscriba steps in—and our customers' stories show just how much of a difference it can make.

Our customers include mid-to-large businesses across indus-tries like technology, e-commerce, financial services, and healthcare. They don't just use Subscriba; they partner with us to transform their approach to SaaS management.

Take Alex, a CFO at a fast-growing e-commerce company, who was facing budget overruns due to hidden subscription renewals and overlapping software licenses. By using Subscriba, Alex's team not only eliminated redundant tools but forecasted future spending with confidence, saving the company thousands in unnecessary costs.

Or consider Priya, an IT manager at a global healthcare provider. With Subscriba's automated renewal reminders and user utilisation insights, Priya's team avoided last-minute contract renewals and right-sized their SaaS stack, ensuring they paid only for what they needed. "Subscriba turned our chaos into clarity," Priya said.

These are just a few of the real stories that show how Subscriba turns a complex process into a strategic advantage. Our customers don't just get data; they get insights that empower better decisions and build trust across their organisations.

Join the growing community of leaders who use Subscriba to simplify, optimise, and excel in their SaaS management journey.

This version tells a story. It opens with a relatable scenario to engage the reader and uses specific customer examples, like Alex and Priya, to create an emotional and human connection. This approach builds trust by showing how real people have successfully used Subscriba to overcome their challenges. The testimonials and direct quotes add authenticity, making the content more credible and memorable.

By employing storytelling and emotional engagement, the optimised version turns a standard customer overview into a page that builds trust and demonstrates Subscriba's impact on a deeper level. It invites readers to imagine their own success with Subscriba, strengthening the brand's position as not just a tool, but a trusted partner in their journey.

Are your marketing messages connecting with your audience's emotions or just skimming the surface with cold, hard facts? If your content isn't engaging hearts as well as minds, you're missing out on powerful connections. Review your last campaign and ask: Does it evoke emotion? If not, rework it to resonate.

Chapter 3
The 7 Archetypal Stories and Their Application in Business Writing

Every great story follows a blueprint. From ancient myths to Hollywood blockbusters, narratives that capture our attention often share fundamental structures that resonate deeply with us. Why? Because these structures are rooted in the human experience, tapping into shared emotions and universal truths.

Believe it or not, there are only seven stories in the world, and every narrative you've ever read, watched, or heard fits into one of these archetypal moulds. Whether it's *Cinderella*, the classic tale of rags to riches, or *The Lord of the Rings*, the quintessential hero's journey, these story structures are embedded in our collective consciousness. They resonate because they're familiar, timeless, and tap into deep-seated human emotions. From Shakespeare's *Macbeth* as a tale of tragedy to *Jaws* as an overcoming-the-monster story, understanding these seven archetypes isn't just an exercise in literary theory, it's a powerful tool for shaping your brand's narrative. Mastering these archetypes can make your messaging more relatable, memorable, and impactful. So, which of these seven stories is your brand telling?

This chapter dives into the seven archetypal stories and explores how you can use them to supercharge your business writing. These are your secret weapons to transform mundane content into gripping stories that connect and convert.

1. Overcoming the Monster

This is the classic story of heroism—think *David and Goliath* or modern tales like *A Quiet Place*. The hero faces a great challenge or threat and overcomes it, emerging stronger. In business, the "monster" could be a common industry problem or a specific challenge your customers face.

Show your customers as the heroes battling a pressing issue, with your product or service as the tool that helps them triumph. For example, Subscriba could craft a story of a finance team drowning in SaaS chaos who, armed with Subscriba, vanquish inefficiencies and cut costs.

2. Rags to Riches

The beloved underdog story. This narrative follows a protagonist who rises from obscurity to greatness—think *Slumdog Millionaire* or *The Pursuit of Happyness*. It's relatable and aspirational, reminding us that transformation is possible.

Use this archetype to highlight your brand's origin story or to showcase a client's journey from struggle to success. A small startup that scaled to industry leader status with Subscriba's help, for instance, makes for a compelling rags-to-riches tale.

3. The Quest

Here, the hero sets out on a journey with a clear goal but faces obstacles along the way. *Star Wars* is a perfect example. The quest archetype taps into our desire for purpose and adventure, making it ideal for stories about dedication and perseverance.

Position your customers or your brand as the hero on a quest for improvement. Maybe Subscriba's "quest" is to bring transparency and optimisation to SaaS management, or a company's mission to streamline processes becomes their journey, with Subscriba as their guiding map.

4. Voyage and Return

In this story, the hero ventures into an unknown world and then returns home, changed by the experience. Think *Alice's Adventures in Wonderland* or *The Wizard of Oz*. This archetype is about exploration, learning, and transformation.

This can be an excellent way to show how customers took a risk, tried Subscriba, and came back with newfound efficiency and control over their SaaS environment. The journey demonstrates growth and learning, positioning your product as the pivotal experience that changed everything.

5. Comedy

Comedy doesn't necessarily mean funny. It's about stories where misunderstandings and confusion give way to harmony and happy endings. *Much Ado About Nothing* and nearly all rom-coms use this structure well. The core element here is conflict that resolves in a satisfying way.

Business content can use the comedy archetype to show how initially complex and disjointed processes (like subscription management) can become seamless and unified. A story about a chaotic IT department that found clarity with Subscriba could fit here, ending on a light-hearted note that reinforces positivity.

6. Tragedy

While you might not think tragedy has a place in business storytelling, it can be powerful when used cautiously. Tragedy stories explore the consequences of mistakes, showing how failure comes from poor choices or missed opportunities. Think *Macbeth* or even business cases where companies faced downfall due to ignoring trends or innovations.

Use the tragedy archetype to show what happens without your product. A story that highlights a business that struggled with SaaS sprawl, ignored the signs, and lost money can act as a cautionary tale that emphasises the value of Subscriba. Be careful with this—end it on a note that offers hope or redemption (hinting at your product as the solution).

7. Rebirth

This is the story of transformation, where the protagonist changes dramatically for the better. Think *A Christmas Carol*, where Scrooge's journey transforms him from miserly to kind-hearted. It's about second chances and redemption.

Rebirth is ideal for customer testimonials and case studies. Show a company that struggled with SaaS inefficiencies until they discovered Subscriba, leading to a dramatic improvement in performance, cost management, and overall satisfaction. This story type fosters hope and portrays your brand as the catalyst for positive change.

Why These Archetypes Work

These archetypes tap into fundamental human emotions and experiences, making them universally relatable. They provide a framework that your audience's brains are already wired to engage with and remember. When you structure your business stories using one of these seven archetypes, you elevate your content from mere information to a narrative that resonates and sticks.

Putting It All Together

Incorporating these archetypal stories into your business writing doesn't mean reinventing your entire content strategy. It's about weaving storytelling into existing content, enhancing everything from case studies to marketing campaigns. Whether you're presenting Subscriba's customer success stories, building an email campaign, or pitching to potential clients, remember that a story is only as compelling as the structure it follows. In this content example, let's look at an email Subscriba's commercial team want to send as part of an ABM (Account Based Marketing) campaign to a qualified ICP (Ideal Customer Profile):

> *Subject Line: Regain Control of Your SaaS Subscriptions*
> *Body: Dear [Name],*
> *Managing SaaS subscriptions can be a daunting task, especially when multiple teams are involved. Subscriba is designed to simplify your subscription management by centralising all your SaaS data in one easy-to-use dashboard. Our platform offers features like real-time cost monitoring, automated renewal reminders, and user utilisation insights to help you optimise your technology spend.*
>
> *Join other industry leaders who have improved their SaaS management and reduced costs with Subscriba.*
> *Schedule a demo today to see how Subscriba can benefit your team.*

This email is clear, informative, and provides an overview of Subscriba's features. However, it lacks emotional pull and urgency. It reads like a typical sales email that most recipients will skim and ignore unless they're already actively seeking a solution. What if Subscriba choose to use the tragedy archetype to engage the reader emotionally:

Subject Line: Don't Let SaaS Mismanagement Cost You Millions

Body: Dear [Name],

Imagine this: A fast-growing company, thriving in all the right ways—until overlooked SaaS renewals and unused licenses turned into a silent drain on their budget. What started as minor inefficiencies snowballed into wasted expenditure and missed opportunities for reinvestment. The CFO realised too late that hidden costs had eroded their bottom line, costing the company hundreds of thousands.

This could have been avoided.

Subscriba is more than just a subscription tracker; it's your safety net. Our platform helps you spot underutilised licenses, alerts you before costly auto-renewals, and provides full visibility across your SaaS landscape—keeping your budget where it belongs: invested in growth, not inefficiencies.

Don't wait until it's too late. Schedule a demo today and see how Subscriba can transform your SaaS management and safeguard your budget.

Your future self will thank you.

Utilising the tragedy archetype paints a relatable picture of what can go wrong without proper SaaS management, triggering the reader's fear of loss—a powerful motivator. The email uses storytelling to build urgency, positioning Subscriba as the hero that prevents a preventable disaster. This not only builds trust but also makes the benefits of Subscriba tangible and impactful.

This email tells a story that resonates on a personal level, prompting the reader to act not just because of what Subscriba offers, but because of what they stand to lose if they don't. This approach makes the email memorable and more likely to generate a response.

Are you using archetypal stories to frame your content—or are you just throwing out a list of features and jargon hoping they stick? Identify an upcoming piece of communication and choose an archetype to shape it. Craft a narrative that makes your audience the hero or warns of a common pitfall. Make it a story they can see themselves in.

Chapter 4
The Hero's Journey in Business – Applying Classic Narratives

Every epic story shares a backbone that resonates deeply with audiences: the Hero's Journey. You've seen it play out in movies, books, and even myths passed down through generations. But what if I told you that this same structure could be the secret weapon that transforms your business writing from dull to dynamic? If you think that sounds far-fetched, stay with me. The Hero's Journey is more than a narrative device; it's a psychological roadmap that mirrors our own experiences, making it one of the most effective storytelling frameworks for your brand.

What Is the Hero's Journey?

The Hero's Journey, popularised by Joseph Campbell, is a narrative structure that follows a hero as they venture out, face challenges, and return transformed. It's broken down into stages: the call to adventure, the trials, the climax, and the return. It's the story arc that turns ordinary people into heroes—and it's more relevant to your business than you might think.

Applying the Hero's Journey to Your Business Story

How does this epic narrative translate to business writing? Simple. Your customer is the hero, not your brand. The hero (your customer) starts with a challenge or problem. They're called to action and meet obstacles along the way. Enter your brand, not as the hero, but as the *mentor* or *guide*—the Yoda to their Luke Skywalker, the Gandalf to their Frodo. Your role is to provide the tools, knowledge, or support that helps them conquer their challenge. When they succeed, your brand is part of their success story.

The Stages of the Hero's Journey in Business Content

Let's break down how each stage applies to your business writing.

1. The Ordinary World

This is the status quo where your customer begins. In your content, paint a picture of the everyday challenges your audience faces. For Subscriba, this could be the chaos of a Head of Procurement juggling multiple SaaS subscriptions with no clear visibility into costs or usage. Make this relatable; it sets the stage for empathy and understanding.

2. The Call to Adventure

This is where your customer recognises a problem and realises, they need to act. Highlight the pain points that trigger the need for change. Maybe it's a story about a finance team that got hit with a surprise six-figure auto-renewal fee because they didn't have the right tools to manage their subscriptions. This is where the stakes are established and the need for a solution becomes urgent.

3. Refusal of the Call

Even heroes hesitate. In business terms, this is where your potential customers may feel overwhelmed or doubtful about taking the first step to solve their problem. They may not even realise how serious or widespread the issue is. Your content should address these hesitations head-on. Maybe a potential Subscriba customer thinks, "Can we really switch from our current tech stack?" Acknowledge these concerns to show you understand them.

4. Meeting the Mentor

Here's where your brand comes in. Position your product or service as the trusted guide that provides the resources and wisdom your customer needs to move forward. Show how Subscriba steps in with its all-in-one SaaS management dashboard, helping CFOs regain control and see the light at the end of the tunnel.

5. Crossing the Threshold

This is where your customer decides to take the plunge and use your product or service. It's a leap of faith. Highlight stories where other customers have taken this step and experienced positive outcomes. Real-life success stories or testimonials can work wonders here to reassure your audience that they're making the right choice.

6. Tests, Allies, and Enemies

Once your customer is onboard, they'll face smaller challenges, like learning how to fully utilise Subscriba's features or dealing with internal pushback from other departments. This is where you show-case your ongoing support—customer service, onboarding materials, and helpful resources. Reinforce that you're still there, guiding them through the trials.

7. The Approach and Ordeal

This stage is where things come to a head. The customer faces the biggest challenge or the most significant test of your product's value. Maybe it's an upcoming budget review or a major SaaS contract renewal negotiation. Your content should illustrate how your product helps them tackle this challenge, giving them both visibility and control, showing its real-world effectiveness.

8. The Reward

Victory! Your customer overcomes the challenge, thanks in part to your product. This is where you showcase the payoff, whether it's money saved, headaches avoided, or processes streamlined. Reinforce their success with metrics, case studies, or user-generated content that highlights the tangible benefits.

9. The Return with the Elixir

The hero returns to their ordinary world, but they're changed for the better. For your customer, this means moving forward with newfound confidence and a streamlined SaaS management system. Your content should close the loop by emphasising how this journey has equipped them to face future challenges with ease, thanks to the ongoing support of your brand.

The Hero's Journey is effective because it taps into deeply ingrained patterns of how we process stories. It doesn't just inform—it takes your audience on an emotional journey that mirrors their real-life experiences. When your customer feels like the hero of their story, and your brand is the trusted mentor, you build trust, loyalty, and a lasting relationship.

Look at your current marketing materials. Are you positioning your brand as the hero or the guide? Flip the script. Make your customers the centre of your story and watch how it transforms engagement. Whether it's in a case study, an ad campaign, or a simple social media post, using the Hero's Journey framework makes your content more compelling and relatable. For our content example let's look at a customer case study.

Case Study: Improving SaaS Management for TechCorp

[Background:]TechCorp, a mid-sized tech company, was struggling with managing its growing number of SaaS subscriptions. With multiple departments subscribing to different services, it was difficult to keep track of costs, contract renewals, and user utilisation.

(Challenge:) The finance team found it challenging to gain visibility into the company's total SaaS spend, leading to duplicate subscriptions and unexpected auto-renewals. This situation resulted in wasted budget and inefficiencies.

[Solution:] TechCorp implemented Subscriba to centralise their SaaS management. With Subscriba's comprehensive dashboard, the company was able to track subscriptions, set renewal alerts, and monitor user utilisation effectively.

[Outcome:] After integrating Subscriba, TechCorp reduced its SaaS costs by 15%, eliminated redundant tools, and improved the overall efficiency of its SaaS management process. The finance team was satisfied with the increased visibility and control over the tech budget.

[Conclusion:]Subscriba helped TechCorp streamline its SaaS operations, leading to cost savings and better financial management.

This case study presents the facts in a straightforward manner. It highlights the problem, solution, and outcome, but lacks emotional engagement and relatability. While it provides information, it reads like a checklist, making it less memorable and impactful.

This alternative version shows what happens if Subscriba leverages the Hero's Journey structure to transform the narrative into an engaging story.

> ***Case Study: How TechCorp Triumphed Over SaaS Chaos with Subscriba***
>
> ***[The Ordinary World]*** *TechCorp, a thriving mid-sized tech company, was moving fast. Departments were innovating, expanding, and adopting new SaaS tools to boost productivity. But behind the scenes, chaos was brewing. The finance team struggled to maintain visibility over a growing number of subscriptions, leading to overlapping services and mounting, unnoticed costs.*
>
> ***[The Call to Adventure]*** *The tipping point came when TechCorp was hit with an unexpected six-figure auto-renewal fee. The finance director, Maya, realised that their SaaS management system—or lack thereof—was unsustainable. It was time to find a solution.*
>
> ***[Refusal of the Call]*** *At first, Maya was hesitant. Implementing a new system felt daunting, and the team questioned if the change was worth the disruption. They feared it would take too much time and effort without guaranteeing results.*
>
> ***[Meeting the Mentor]*** *That's when Subscriba entered the picture. Maya was introduced to Subscriba's comprehensive dashboard—a platform that promised to bring order to their SaaS chaos. With features like automated renewal alerts, cost tracking, and user utilisation insights, Subscriba was more than just a tool; it was a guide ready to lead TechCorp out of its SaaS maze.*
>
> ***[Crossing the Threshold]*** *With some initial reservations, Maya's team decided to take the plunge and implement Subscriba. The onboarding process was smoother than*

expected, with Subscriba's support team guiding them every step of the way.

[Tests, Allies, and Enemies] The first challenge came when the IT department flagged a potential issue with duplicate services. With Subscriba's real-time insights, Maya and her team were able to identify and consolidate overlapping subscriptions. Departments initially pushed back, but Subscriba's custom reports helped demonstrate the benefits of the changes, turning sceptics into allies.

[The Approach and Ordeal] The ultimate test arrived during the company's annual budget review. Would the changes show a significant impact? Tensions were high as the team prepared reports and presentations backed by Subscriba's detailed analytics.

[The Reward] The results were beyond expectations. TechCorp's SaaS costs had been reduced by 15%, and unused licenses were cut, leading to an overall savings of $200,000 that could be reinvested in growth. The finance team celebrated their newfound clarity and control, and Maya earned recognition for leading the charge.

[The Return with the Elixir] Today, TechCorp operates with streamlined SaaS management and improved cost control. Maya's team has the confidence and tools to handle future SaaS expansions without fear of hidden surprises. Thanks to Subscriba, TechCorp's SaaS management went from a financial liability to a strategic advantage.

If you'd like our team to help you transform chaos into clarity, Contact us today

By positioning TechCorp's finance director as the hero, it humanises the story and creates a journey the reader can relate to. Subscriba is positioned as the mentor, providing the tools and support needed to succeed. Each stage builds anticipation and emotional engagement, making the reader invested in the outcome. The ending is satisfying and demonstrates transformation, which reinforces trust in Subscriba as a partner rather than just a product.

This approach makes the case study more compelling, memorable, and shareable. It shows that Subscriba doesn't just offer features; it delivers impactful change, positioning the product as essential and valuable.

Chapter 5
Creating Relatable Characters – Your Brand as a Protagonist

Let's face it: in the world of business storytelling, brands often take centre stage in the wrong way. They position themselves as the heroes, doing everything, saving the day, and expecting applause. But here's the truth—no one cares about a perfect hero, especially when it's a brand. People don't connect with faultless protagonists; they connect with relatable ones that remind them of themselves. To create stories that resonate, your brand needs to become a protagonist that your audience can understand, root for, and see as human.

Why Relatable Characters Matter

A relatable character isn't just a nice-to-have; it's the glue that binds your audience to your story. Why? Because when people see themselves in a character, they become emotionally invested. Think about it: you're not going to lean into a story where the hero is untouchable, flawless, and never struggles. But show them facing setbacks, doubts, or relatable challenges, and suddenly you're rooting for them. This is true whether your character is a person or, in this case, your brand.

To build a brand that resonates, you need to create a character that feels real, relatable, and human. One key element is vulnerability. Perfection may seem desirable, but it doesn't resonate—imperfection does. When a brand admits it doesn't have all the answers or shares moments of learning and growth, it becomes approachable. Brands that openly discuss how they adapted through tough times build trust, inviting audiences to relate to them on a personal level.

Another essential component is personality. A relatable brand is more than just a logo and a tagline; it has a voice, tone, and set of characteristics that define it. Whether your brand's voice is witty, empathetic, or bold, it should remain consistent across all channels. This consistency helps reinforce the brand's identity and makes it familiar to its audience, fostering a stronger connection.

Shared values are also crucial. Your audience is far more likely to connect with your brand if it stands for something they care about. If your brand is passionate about issues like sustainability, diversity, or innovation, let those values be a central part of your stories. When people see their own beliefs reflected in your brand, they don't just engage with it—they align with it.

Lastly, growth and evolution make a brand relatable. Just like the most compelling characters in stories learn and change, so should your brand. Show how your brand has adapted, learned from challenges, or evolved over time. Whether it's a product pivot that responded to customer needs or an improved customer service strategy that came from feedback, sharing that journey demonstrates that your brand is dynamic and responsive, making it more human and relatable.

Turning Your Brand into a Relatable Protagonist

Here's how to apply these principles to your business storytelling:

Start with a Backstory: Every great character has a backstory, and so should your brand. It's not just about when your company was founded; it's about the "why" behind it. What problem were you trying to solve? What challenges did you face in the beginning? Sharing your brand's origin story adds layers to your character and makes it relatable. For example, Subscriba didn't just appear out of thin air; it was born from the frustration of finance teams and IT managers grappling with SaaS sprawl. By highlighting these roots, you show that your brand understands your customers' pain because it's been there.

Showcase Struggles and Triumphs: A protagonist without struggle is as dull as a meeting that should have been an email. Don't just focus on your brand's wins; highlight the challenges you've faced. Maybe Subscriba once struggled to integrate with certain SaaS platforms or learned the hard way that user feedback is invaluable. These moments of vulnerability make your brand human. People appreciate a brand that can say, "We learned from this, and here's how we've improved."

Give Your Brand a Voice: Imagine reading a book where the main character's voice changes from chapter to chapter. Confusing, right? The same goes for your brand. Your voice should be consistent, reflecting a personality that aligns with your values and your audience's expectations. Is Subscriba supportive and professional or tech-savvy and playful? The tone you choose should remain steady, making your brand instantly recognisable.

Make Your Brand's Journey Visible: People love to watch a character grow, and they love to see brands do the same. Share milestones, product updates, and even setbacks. Maybe Subscriba once pivoted its strategy based on customer feedback or partnered with another platform to offer better integration. Each step is part of your brand's story and adds depth to your character. The goal is to show evolution, demonstrating that your brand isn't static but alive, learning, and adapting.

Look at brands that do this well: Apple's story isn't just about sleek products; it's about the relentless pursuit of innovation after early failures. Patagonia isn't just an outdoor clothing company; it's a brand with a deep commitment to environmental sustainability, showcased through stories of both successes and lessons learned.

Now, think about how your brand can follow suit. Maybe Subscriba's story involves an early struggle to onboard its first big client and how that experience shaped its customer support philosophy. By sharing these narratives, your audience sees a brand that's not only capable but relatable and approachable.

Take a fresh look at your content. Does it portray your brand as a polished, untouchable hero, or does it show the ups and downs that make it relatable? Does your brand's story have vulnerability, personality, shared values, and visible growth? If not, it's time to rework it. Start small—introduce a story about a lesson learned or a challenge overcome and see how your audience responds.

As we move forward, keep this in mind: relatable characters drive engagement because they reflect the real, imperfect journeys we all take. Your brand's story shouldn't just tell people what you do; it should show them who you are and why they should care. And that, is how you use storytelling to turn your brand into a protagonist worth rooting for. In this content example, we'll look at a social media post to remind customers that the company will be having its annual all-hands meeting and as a result, there will be limited tech support:

> **Caption:** *Reminder: Our team will be hosting an annual all-hands meeting next Friday. Emergency tech support will still be available, but response times may be slightly delayed. Thank you for your understanding and patience.*
> **Image:** *Company logo with text that reads: "Annual All-Hands Meeting Next Friday. Emergency Tech Support Available."*

The post is clear and informative, but it's very formal and lacks personality. It simply delivers the facts without fostering any connection with the audience. While it communicates the necessary information, it does little to engage or make the reader feel involved in the company's culture. Now let's try the same social post but this time positioning the brand as a relatable character:

> **Caption:** *Next Friday is an exciting day for our team—it's our annual all-hands meeting! This is when we come together to celebrate milestones, share insights, and plan for an even brighter future. But don't worry, we've got you covered! While our full team will be diving into company growth and bonding, we know that emergencies don't take a day off. That's why we're ensuring emergency tech support will still be available.*
>
> *A heads-up: response times might be a little slower than usual, so we appreciate your patience and understanding. We'll be back at full speed with renewed energy and ideas to better serve you.*
>
> *Have questions or an urgent matter next Friday? Drop us a message, and our dedicated emergency team will be there for you.*
> **Image:** *A friendly, behind-the-scenes photo of the team or a visual that reads: "Annual All-Hands Meeting Next Friday. Emergency Support Still Available!"*

By framing the all-hands meeting as an exciting event, the post humanises the company, giving followers a glimpse into its culture. The tone is warm and friendly, acknowledging the audience's needs while sharing what's happening behind the scenes. The post also uses inclusive language ("we," "our team," "we appreciate your patience"), which invites the reader to feel like part of the company's journey.

This approach builds trust and connection by showing that the company has personality and values its customers. It also sets clear expectations while making the audience feel considered, not just informed. This turns a routine update into an engaging narrative that reinforces the brand's identity and relatability.

Does your brand come across as relatable and human, or is it just a faceless entity? Review this week's social media posts. Are you showcasing your brand's personality, growth, and shared values? Or is it corporate waffle? Add a touch of vulnerability or a real moment to connect with your audience today.

Chapter 6
Setting the Scene – Context Matters

Imagine opening a book to find the first line reads, "The protagonist solved the mystery." Intriguing? Hardly. There's no backdrop, no hint of a story to latch onto. In business storytelling, the scene sets the stage for everything that follows. It provides context, frames the problem, and invites your audience to care. Without it, even the most compelling stories fall flat, devoid of relatability or urgency.

So, what does "setting the scene" mean for your brand's content? It means giving your audience enough information to understand the stakes and become invested in the journey. Let's break down why context matters and how you can use it to elevate your content from a dry recitation of facts to an immersive experience that sticks.

Why Context is King

Context gives meaning. It transforms a statement from noise into something that resonates. Think about it—saying, "Our product increases productivity by 30%" is a strong claim, but without context, it's just a number. Now imagine starting with: "Imagine you're an IT manager whose team is drowning in tools that barely communicate with each other. You're juggling software, deadlines, and a shrinking budget. That's where we stepped in..." Suddenly, that 30% productivity boost has relevance. It's more than just a number; it's the answer to a real problem.

Context is what turns facts into stories. It sets the stakes, frames the problem, and positions your brand as the trusted guide. Without it, your audience has no reason to invest emotionally or mentally in what you're telling them.

To create a scene that truly captures your audience's attention, start by setting the environment. Where is your story unfolding? Is it in the fast-paced world of a startup where every second counts, or within the meticulous, detail-oriented confines of a finance department? Paint the picture vividly enough that your audience can imagine themselves in it, feeling the energy or tension of the space.

Next, consider the stakes. Why should your audience care? What's on the line if the problem isn't addressed? Show the potential consequences, whether it's missed opportunities, wasted resources, or a significant financial setback. This is where you build the tension that keeps your audience invested and eager for a resolution—ideally, one that your brand provides.

Then, introduce the characters. Who is this story about? Whether it's a specific customer, a team, or an entire department, ensure they're relatable. Instead of making a vague statement like, "Many companies struggle with SaaS management," bring it to life: "Meet Lisa, a procurement manager who spends her days juggling dozens of SaaS contracts and her nights worrying about overlooked renewals." Characters like Lisa pull your audience in, helping them see their own challenges reflected in the narrative.

Finally, outline the problem with clarity. What is the specific challenge your character is facing? Is it the unexpected costs of underutilised software? Is it the chaos of managing multiple renewals and deadlines scattered across different tools? The more vividly you describe the problem, the more invested your audience will be in seeing how it's resolved.

Building Context in Business Writing

When applying this to your content, don't just jump into how great your product or service is. Frame the story first. For Subscriba, that might mean painting a scene of a company grappling with subscription sprawl, their finance team frantically piecing together data from spreadsheets, emails, and scattered documents. Then, introduce your product as the much-needed solution to this overwhelming mess.

Consider these questions when setting the scene:

- Who is experiencing this problem?
- What's their day-to-day like before they find your solution?
- What emotions or reactions do they have to their current situation?
- What's at stake if nothing changes?

Answering these questions doesn't just set the stage; it makes your story relatable and engaging.

The Power of Context in Action

Let's look at an example. A generic statement like, "Subscriba helps manage SaaS subscriptions," is informative but bland. Now, add context:

"It's the end of the month, and Greg, the finance director, is hunched over his desk, surrounded by a labyrinth of spreadsheets and notes. The company's SaaS renewals are due, and one overlooked contract could cost thousands. This was Greg's life before Subscriba— a stressful juggling act with stakes too high to ignore."

Suddenly, the solution matters more. The audience relates to Greg's stress and understands why Subscriba's features are valuable. Context makes the story stick.

Common Pitfalls and How to Avoid Them

Too Much Detail: While context is crucial, avoid drowning your audience in minutiae. Set the scene, but leave enough room for the main story to breathe.

Generic Backdrops: Saying "many businesses" or "lots of teams" doesn't engage. Specifics do. Use real or composite characters that represent your target audience.

Rushing to the Solution: Resist the urge to fast-forward to your product. Building up the scene creates anticipation and makes the reveal of your solution more satisfying.

Takeaways for Your Brand

Every piece of content you create—from case studies to social media posts—should start by setting the scene. Make your audience feel the urgency, relate to the characters, and understand the stakes before you introduce your brand as the guide. Whether you're crafting a blog post, an email campaign, or a video script, setting the scene is what hooks your audience and makes them care.

As you review your current content, ask yourself: Are you setting the stage or simply stating facts? Remember, a well-set scene isn't just an introduction; it's an invitation for your audience to step into the story and see how your brand fits into their journey.

In the following content example let's look at an email to announce a new feature that enables users to connect and track offline subscriptions:

> **Subject Line:** *New Feature Alert: Track Offline Subscriptions with Subscriba*
> **Body:** *Dear [Name],*
> *We're excited to announce our latest feature! Subscriba now enables users to connect and track offline subscriptions such as professional memberships, staff gym memberships, trade*

magazine subscriptions, and more. This new feature helps you gain complete visibility over all types of expenses, ensuring you stay in control of both online and offline subscriptions.

Discover how Subscriba's comprehensive dashboard can now make managing offline subscriptions as seamless as your SaaS tools.

Ready to streamline your subscription tracking even further? Log in now to explore this new capability or schedule a demo to see it in action.

The communication is straightforward and informative, clearly outlining the new feature. However, it falls short in emotional appeal and engagement. It comes across as a generic update that could easily be overlooked or skimmed without creating genuine interest or a sense of urgency. Look what happens when we set the scene with relatable context.

Subject Line: Is Your Budget Leaking? New Feature to Track Hidden Subscriptions
Body: Dear [Name],
Picture this: The end of the quarter is here, and you're finalising your budget. You meticulously review every SaaS subscription and licence fee. You breathe a sigh of relief—everything checks out. But then, you glance at a line item that always slips through the cracks: offline subscriptions. Those professional memberships, employee gym passes, and trade magazine renewals quietly eating away at your budget without visibility.

This is where Subscriba's new feature steps in. We're thrilled to introduce our latest upgrade: the ability to connect and track offline subscriptions seamlessly alongside your digital ones. Whether it's staff training memberships, industry-specific publications, or personal employee perks, Subscriba now ensures that no subscription goes unnoticed.

With this new capability, you can manage all your expenses in one place, so those hidden costs don't turn into end-of-quarter surprises. Say goodbye to budget leaks and hello to comprehensive control.

Ready to experience this game-changing feature? Log in today or schedule a demo to see how it can work for you.

By painting a picture of a finance professional's end-of-quarter review and the stress of finding hidden expenses, the email captures the reader's attention and makes the new feature feel immediately relevant. It uses specific examples of offline subscriptions that resonate with the target audience, illustrating why this feature is valuable. The tone is engaging, and the message builds urgency by positioning the new feature as the solution to a familiar, frustrating problem. It transforms a simple product announcement into a relatable story that speaks directly to the audience's experiences, making them more likely to act.

Chapter 7

The Importance of Conflict and Resolution – Driving Engagement

Stories without conflict are like songs without a beat—flat and forgettable. Conflict isn't just an optional add-on in storytelling; it's the driving force that keeps your audience engaged. Without conflict, there's no journey, no emotional pull, and certainly no reason for readers to stay invested until the end. But what does this mean for your business writing? It means you need to show the stakes, present challenges, and reveal how your product or service is the resolution that delivers the payoff.

Why Conflict Matters

Think about the stories that grab your attention. They don't start with, "Everything was perfect, and it stayed that way." They start with tension—whether it's a hero facing an uphill battle, a team overcoming obstacles, or a business wrestling with an industry-wide problem. Conflict engages because it's relatable. Your audience knows what it's like to face challenges, so they'll pay attention when you show them how you or your customers have done the same.

In business content, conflict sets up the need for a solution. If you're showcasing a case study, the problem a customer faced is the conflict. If you're drafting an email campaign, the obstacle that's holding back your audience's success is the conflict. This isn't about being negative; it's about being realistic. People want to know that you understand their pain points before you pitch a solution.

The Anatomy of Conflict in Business Stories

Here's how to use conflict effectively in your business storytelling:

Be Specific: Generic challenges don't stick. Instead of saying, "Our customers faced issues with inefficiencies," say, "Our client, a mid-sized tech firm, found themselves tangled in a web of SaaS subscriptions that led to unexpected costs and a 10% budget overrun."

Relatability is Key: The conflict you present should resonate with your target audience. If you're speaking to CFOs, highlight budget constraints, surprise expenses, or inefficient processes. If your audience is IT managers, focus on the chaos of software sprawl, siloed data, or integration headaches.

Highlight the Stakes: What happens if the conflict isn't resolved? Will the business lose money, miss growth opportunities, or jeopardise team productivity? Make it clear why the problem is pressing. This primes your audience to care about the resolution.

Resolution: The Reward Your Audience Craves

Conflict by itself isn't enough. Without a resolution, your story leaves your audience hanging, frustrated, and disconnected. Resolution provides the satisfaction that makes a story worthwhile and solidifies your brand's role as the trusted guide.

For Subscriba, the resolution could be the introduction of a feature that turns chaos into clarity, like automated renewal alerts that saved a client thousands of dollars in unexpected fees. The key is to show how your product or service resolved the conflict and improved the customer's situation. This demonstrates your value in a relatable, memorable way.

Creating Resolution That Sticks

To write a compelling resolution, keep these pointers in mind:

Be Concrete: Just as you need to be specific with the conflict, your resolution should include tangible outcomes. "After implementing Subscriba, the finance team regained control of their budget, saving 15% on SaaS costs and eliminating redundant subscriptions" is more powerful than "We helped them improve efficiency."

Show Transformation: Highlight how your customer's situation changed after using your solution. What did they learn? How did their day-to-day operations improve? A resolution is most effective when it feels earned—when it shows that a journey took place, and the customer came out better on the other side.

End on a Positive Note: Your resolution should leave your audience with a sense of possibility and optimism. Even if your story focuses on a tough challenge, it should end with hope, progress, or a key takeaway that the reader can apply.

Conflict and Resolution in Different Content Types

Let's look at how you can use conflict and resolution across various types of business content:

Case Studies: Outline the specific challenges your client faced (the conflict), the turning point when they discovered your product, and the measurable success they achieved (the resolution).

Email Campaigns: Start with a relatable pain point, such as managing subscription renewals manually (the conflict), and introduce your tool as the solution that simplifies the process (the resolution).

Blog Posts: Present a common industry challenge or misconception and guide the reader through the journey of overcoming it, with your product or expertise providing the resolution.

Social Media Posts: Use short-form storytelling to hook your audience with a problem and provide a glimpse of the resolution that encourages them to engage further, such as visiting your site or reading a full case study.

The Emotional Arc: Why it Works

Conflict and resolution mirror real-life experiences. Your audience has faced struggles and understands the emotional payoff that comes with finding a solution. This familiarity with the emotional arc is why storytelling feels so natural and why people stay engaged. By structuring your content around a clear conflict and a rewarding resolution, you're tapping into a narrative pattern that's been proven to work for centuries.

Conflict is what pulls your audience into your story, and resolution is what keeps them coming back. Without both, your content is just another forgettable piece in the endless sea of information. So, look at your current content—are you setting up conflicts that your audience relates to and resolving them in a way that showcases your value? If not, it's time to rework your approach and bring your stories to life with conflict and resolution. Your audience will thank you for it. In this content example we'll look at a social media post about companies paying for under-utilised tools:

> **Caption:** *Managing SaaS subscriptions can be a complex and costly task. With Subscriba, businesses can identify under-utilised tools and optimise their tech stack. One of our clients, TechCorp, was able to replace four third-party platforms with two and reduce the number of licences required, thanks to Subscriba's comprehensive dashboard.*

*Want to optimise your SaaS spending? Find out how
Subscriba can help.*
Image: *A simple graphic of a dashboard with text that reads:
"Cut Costs, Simplify Subscriptions."*

The post states the facts and outcome but lacks the storytelling
elements that would make the content more relatable and
compelling. There's no conflict to draw the reader in, and the resolution feels disconnected from any real challenge. This time we want to
re-write it by leaning into the conflict and resolution:

Caption: *Picture this: A CFO staring at an ever-growing
spreadsheet, full of overlapping SaaS tools and redundant
licences. Frustration mounts as budget meetings loom, and he
knows something has to give.*

*Enter Subscriba. Using our platform, this CFO didn't just
identify the under-utilised software lurking in the tech stack;
he acted. By analysing crossover features, he streamlined the
company's subscriptions from four third-party platforms to
just two, slashing redundant licences and saving thousands.*

*The result? A more efficient, cost-effective tech landscape and
a CFO who can finally breathe easier.*

Does your SaaS landscape need a closer look? Let's talk.
Image: *A dynamic image showing an overlapping Venn
diagram of SaaS tools with "Identified and Optimised" highlighted in the middle, or a visual representation of reduction
(e.g., arrows going from four to two).*

This time we're setting the scene by creating a relatable scenario for
the target audience—a stressed CFO facing a familiar challenge. This
introduction adds context and conflict that the reader can empathise

with, making the story more engaging. The post then moves smoothly into the resolution, showing how Subscriba helped solve the problem and presenting a tangible outcome (streamlined subscriptions and cost savings). The call to action ("Does your SaaS landscape need a closer look? Let's talk") prompts engagement while positioning Subscriba as the solution.

By leveraging storytelling elements that drive engagement, we're making the audience feel seen and understood. It turns a simple case study into a narrative journey, reinforcing the value of Subscriba in a relatable and memorable way.

Chapter 8
Emotional Connection – The Heart of Effective Storytelling

When was the last time you read a piece of marketing copy and actually felt something? If the answer is "I don't remember," then you've experienced firsthand why so much content fails. Information is important, sure, but if it doesn't tug at the reader's emotions, it won't stick. Emotional connection isn't just a nice-to-have in story-telling—it's the secret sauce that turns ordinary content into something that engages, resonates, and compels action.

Why Emotions Matter More Than Facts

Here's a truth that many marketers overlook: decisions are emotional first, logical second. People are more likely to make purchasing decisions based on how they feel and then justify those choices with logic afterward. This means that if your story doesn't evoke any emotion, you're missing a crucial opportunity to connect with your audience in a meaningful way.

Emotions are what make stories memorable. You might not remember the technical specs of a product, but you'll remember how it made you feel when you read about it solving a relatable problem.

This is why content that triggers emotional responses—whether it's excitement, relief, empathy, or even concern—leaves a lasting impression.

Types of Emotions That Drive Engagement

Not all emotions are created equal when it comes to storytelling. Here's a look at the types of emotions that can amplify your content:

Empathy: This is the cornerstone of connection. When your audience feels understood, they're more likely to trust you. Show that your brand recognises their challenges, fears, or aspirations, and you'll build a bridge that facts alone can't create.
Excitement: Spark curiosity and anticipation to keep your audience engaged. Whether it's a new feature launch or an exclusive deal, excitement can make your audience eager to act.
Relief: Demonstrating how your product or service solves a pressing problem can evoke a sense of relief. This emotion reassures your audience that you have the answer they've been looking for.
Inspiration: Stories of success, transformation, or overcoming the odds can inspire your audience, positioning your brand as not just a provider but a partner in their journey.

Emotional connection isn't about tugging on heartstrings just for the sake of it. It's about aligning your brand's message with the real emotions your audience experiences. Specifics make emotions come to life. Compare "Our client saw improved results" to "Our client saved 10 hours a week and reduced budget stress, allowing their team to focus on strategic initiatives." The latter paints a picture of the impact and triggers an emotional response. Specifics give your audience something tangible to hold on to, which helps them feel the story on a deeper level.

While emotions are powerful, overdoing them can backfire. If every piece of content is emotionally charged, it loses its authenticity and can feel manipulative. Balance is key. Use emotion strategically, weaving it into your stories where it matters most, like in customer success stories, feature launches, or mission-driven content.

The Power of Humour in Emotional Connection

While empathy, inspiration, and excitement are crucial for creating emotional connections, don't underestimate the power of humour. Used strategically, humour can make your brand more relatable, break down barriers, and foster a sense of camaraderie with your audience. In a world where business content can often be dry and overly serious, a well-placed joke or light-hearted comment can be a breath of fresh air.

But let's be clear: humour should never come at the expense of others. Making fun of competitors, customers, or anyone else can easily backfire and damage your brand's reputation. Instead, self-deprecating humour, when used appropriately, can show humility and build trust. It makes your brand human, showing that you're not above acknowledging mistakes or sharing a laugh at your own expense.

The KFC "FCK" Campaign: A Masterclass in Humorous Storytelling

A prime example of using humour to build emotional connection is KFC's "FCK" campaign in the UK. When KFC faced the monumental problem of running out of chicken—a nightmare for a brand that prides itself on being the king of fried chicken—public criticism and reputational damage seemed inevitable. But instead of a standard corporate apology, KFC leaned into the moment with a bold, self-deprecating response.

The company released an ad showing an empty chicken bucket with their logo rearranged to spell "FCK," followed by a light-hearted yet sincere apology. This move showcased humility and humour, acknowledging their blunder without making excuses. The response was widely praised as a storytelling genius because it turned a crisis into a moment of relatability and connection. It said, "We messed up, we know it, and we're laughing along with you."

Humour is effective because it triggers positive emotions. It's disarming, makes content more shareable, and can turn a potentially negative experience into a moment of connection. When people laugh, they feel good, and they're more likely to associate those positive feelings with your brand.

How to Use Humour Effectively

Be Genuine: Forced jokes or overly scripted humour can fall flat. Let your brand's true personality shine through.
Stay on Brand: Your humour should align with your overall brand voice. If your brand is known for being professional and serious, a sudden attempt at slapstick humour might confuse your audience.
Keep it Light: Simple, friendly humour is best. Avoid anything that could be seen as offensive or divisive.
Self-Deprecation: When used at the right moment, self-deprecating humour can show humility and build trust. The KFC example demonstrates how acknowledging and laughing at your own mistakes can turn potential reputational damage into a public relations win.

Adding Humour to Your Content

Think about how you can weave humour into your brand storytelling without losing professionalism. Whether it's a playful social media post or a light-hearted email, a touch of humour can make your content stand out. For Subscriba, this could mean a humorous take on the common frustrations of SaaS management, like: *"If you're tired of unplanned, unmanaged & unwelcome Software-as-a-Service subscrip-*

tion costs playing havoc with your cost reporting, then it's time to deploy Subscriba."

Humour, when done right, is a powerful tool for creating emotional connection. It shows that your brand has a personality, can acknowledge its own flaws, and is approachable. So, don't be afraid to smile as you craft your content; your audience will be more inclined to smile—and engage—right back.

As you continue to create content, consider how humour might play a role. Could a touch of wit or self-deprecation make your message more engaging? Remember, even the most serious brands can benefit from a moment of levity when it's used thoughtfully.

Chapter 9
Visual and Sensory Language – Bringing Your Story to Life

Words have power, but words that paint a picture are unforgettable. That's the difference between telling a story and making your audience feel like they're living it. Visual and sensory language isn't just a fancy literary tool; it's what transforms dry, lifeless content into an immersive experience. It engages the reader's imagination, triggers emotional responses, and makes your message resonate long after the words are read.

Why Visual and Sensory Language Matters

When someone reads your content, you want them to do more than skim. You want them to pause, imagine, and connect. Sensory language taps into the part of the brain that processes real-life experiences, making your audience feel like they're part of the story. Instead of telling them how great your product is, show them through vivid descriptions that engage their senses.

Consider these two sentences:

1. *"Our platform simplifies your SaaS management process."*
2. *"Imagine a dashboard—a single, clear view where every subscription clicks neatly into place, cutting through the fog of spreadsheets and scattered notes."*

Which one sparks an image in your mind? That's the power of visual and sensory language.

Our brains are wired to respond to sensory input. When we read language that evokes sight, sound, touch, taste, or smell, the sensory cortex of the brain activates, making the experience more vivid. This neurological response helps with recall, which is why stories that incorporate sensory details are remembered far longer than those that don't.

Incorporating sensory language into your content doesn't mean going overboard with flowery descriptions. It means being intentional about word choice to create a richer experience. Here's how to do it:

Use Specific, Concrete Details

Vague language is the enemy of engagement. Instead of saying, "Our dashboard is easy to use," describe what it looks like and how it feels to navigate it: *"With just a glance, you can see your entire tech stack laid out in clean, intuitive panels that invite you to explore."*

Appeal to Multiple Senses

While sight is the most common sense used in writing, don't forget the others. How would your product sound if it had a voice? What texture would it have? For example, if you're describing a feature in Subscriba that alerts users to upcoming renewals, you could write: *"A subtle chime notifies you before an auto-renewal can sneak past, bringing a sense of calm and control to your busy day."*

Create Comparisons

Metaphors and similes can make complex ideas relatable. Instead of "Our platform is reliable," try "Using Subscriba feels as natural as flipping a light switch, instantly illuminating everything you need to know."

Practical Application in Business Writing

How do you use visual and sensory language in everyday business writing?

Case Studies: Don't just state that a company saw improved results. Describe the scene: *"The finance director sat back for the first time in months, seeing the tidy columns of projected savings on the Subscriba dashboard—like puzzle pieces finally snapping into place."*

Emails: Engage your reader by setting a vivid scene: *"Does this sound familiar? It's 6 p.m., and your finance team is scrambling to find renewal dates buried in email threads. With Subscriba, those chaotic evenings turn into a smooth click of a button, as clear and refreshing as the first sip of your morning coffee."*

Blog Posts: When explaining industry trends or challenges, sensory language makes abstract ideas tangible: *"SaaS sprawl isn't just a budget concern; it's a shadow that creeps over your strategy, slowly obscuring clarity and control."*

Social Media: You might think visual and sensory language is too elaborate for short posts, but even a few well-chosen words can make a difference: *"Is your budget buried under the shadow of forgotten software? Bring it to light with Subscriba."*

When Less Is More

While sensory language can elevate your content, balance is key. Too much descriptive language can bog down your writing and make it feel contrived. The goal is to add richness without losing clarity. A few carefully chosen sensory details can do more than a paragraph of over-the-top imagery.

Chapter 10
Voice and Tone – Consistency Across Channels

Imagine meeting someone who seems warm and friendly in person, only to find their emails are cold and robotic. Or reading a light-hearted blog post, then finding the company's LinkedIn page is all corporate jargon. Inconsistent voice and tone can be jarring and, more importantly, erode trust. Your audience should feel like they're interacting with the same brand, no matter where or how they engage with you. This chapter will break down why voice and tone matter, how they differ, and how you can maintain consistency across all your channels.

Voice vs. Tone: What's the Difference?

Before we dive into creating consistency, let's clear up a common confusion: voice and tone. They're related but distinct.

Voice: This is your brand's personality. It's constant and doesn't change. Whether you're witty, empathetic, authoritative, or quirky, your voice should be recognisable in every piece of content. Think of it as your brand's character.

Tone: This is the mood or attitude you take on in specific situations. Unlike voice, tone adapts based on context. Your tone might be more serious when addressing a technical issue but light-hearted in a social media post celebrating a company milestone.

Think of voice as your brand's DNA, and tone as the way that DNA is expressed in different scenarios. Subscriba, for example, may have a supportive and professional voice, but its tone might shift from reassuring (when discussing data security) to playful (when engaging with followers on social media).

Why Consistency Matters

Consistency in voice and tone builds trust and makes your brand instantly recognisable. People are naturally drawn to familiarity, and a consistent voice helps create that. It signals to your audience that they're engaging with the same brand across channels—whether they're reading your blog, checking your website, or scrolling through your social media posts.

Inconsistent voice and tone can make your brand feel fragmented and untrustworthy. Imagine a potential customer who visits your website, finds your blog helpful and conversational, and then receives a cold, formal marketing email. It creates a disconnect that can make them question your brand's authenticity.

Developing Your Brand's Voice and Tone

To establish a consistent voice and adaptable tone, start with these steps:

Define Your Voice
Take the time to clearly outline what your brand voice is—and isn't. This might mean creating a brand voice document that includes:

Adjectives that describe your brand (e.g., supportive, witty, reliable).

Adjectives you want to avoid (e.g., overly casual, arrogant, detached).

Sample sentences that demonstrate your brand's voice in action.

Subscriba's voice could be described as *supportive, insightful, and straightforward*. It doesn't use complicated jargon unless necessary and always aims to make complex SaaS management approachable.

Adapt Your Tone Based on Context

Your tone should adjust depending on the type of content and where it's being posted. Here's how Subscriba's tone might vary:

Website Content: Professional, clear, and informative. The tone should exude confidence and reliability.

Social Media: Friendly, engaging, and slightly more casual. This is where you can let some humour and personality shine through.

Customer Support: Empathetic, calm, and solution-oriented. Customers should feel reassured and understood.

Emails: Tailored to the purpose. A sales email might be direct and persuasive, while a product update email could be excited but professional.

Maintaining Consistency Across Channels

Once you've defined your voice and adaptable tones, the challenge is to keep them consistent across all your content. Here are a few strategies:

Create a Voice and Tone Guide: Document your brand voice and examples of tone variations in a guide that's accessible to everyone involved in content creation. Include dos and don'ts, sample phrases, and scenarios that show how tone should shift. This guide ensures that whether someone is writing a blog post or drafting a tweet, they have a reference to keep the voice aligned.

Train Your Team: Consistency isn't achieved through guidelines alone. Train your content, marketing, and support teams to understand and embody your brand's voice. Workshops, regular reviews, and feedback sessions can help align everyone and make sure your brand's voice remains unified.

Audit Your Content Regularly: It's easy for voice and tone to drift over time, especially as new team members join or priorities shift. Conduct regular audits of your content across all channels to check for consistency. If something feels off, update it to align with your brand voice.

Examples of Consistent Voice and Tone

Imagine Subscriba launches a new feature that tracks offline subscriptions. Here's how consistent voice and adaptable tone could play out across channels:

Website Announcement: "We're excited to introduce a new way to simplify your subscription tracking. With Subscriba's offline subscription feature, you can now manage everything from professional memberships to trade magazines in one place."

Social Media Post: "Ever forgotten to cancel that gym membership? We've all been there. Good news: Subscriba's new offline subscription tracking keeps every detail in one easy view."

Customer Support Email: "Hi [Name], we're happy to share that our new feature lets you manage offline subscriptions effortlessly. If you have any questions, we're here to help walk you through it step-by-step."

Blog Post: "Managing offline subscriptions like trade magazines and gym memberships just got easier. Subscriba's latest feature integrates these expenses seamlessly into your dashboard, helping you maintain a complete overview of your budget."

Notice how the voice remains supportive and informative throughout, while the tone adapts—more enthusiastic for social media, slightly formal for the website, and empathetic in customer support.

While consistency is crucial, remember that different channels and contexts may require a slight tweak in tone. The goal is not to sound robotic but to maintain a unified brand personality that feels natural and relatable in any situation.

A consistent voice is key to ensuring your brand is recognisable and trustworthy across all channels. But what if you haven't yet settled on what that voice should be? Here's a practical task to help you discover it: write the same social media post in five different voices and get feedback from key stakeholders on which voice best reflects your company's DNA. Below are examples of how Subscriba might announce an upcoming CFO roundtable, each in a distinct voice:

Authoritative and Professional: "Join us for Subscriba's exclusive CFO Roundtable, where industry leaders will gather to discuss the latest trends in SaaS management and budgeting strategies. Reserve your spot to gain valuable insights and network with peers. Spaces are limited—register today."

Conversational and Friendly: "Hey CFOs! We know SaaS management can be a maze, so we're hosting a roundtable just for you. Join us for an open chat with fellow finance leaders, share tips, and learn how to navigate your tech stack with ease. Save your seat—it's going to be insightful!"

Witty and Light-Hearted: "Attention CFOs: tired of feeling like a tightrope walker balancing your SaaS budget? Join our Subscriba CFO Roundtable for practical tips, hearty laughs, and real talk on making those renewals less terrifying. Limited seats—grab yours before they vanish!"

Empathetic and Supportive: "We understand the challenges CFOs face with SaaS budgeting and cost control. That's why Subscriba is organising a roundtable to bring together finance leaders to share experiences and solutions. Join us and find your community —where your challenges are understood and your insights matter."

Innovative and Forward-Thinking: "The future of SaaS management is evolving, and so should your strategies. Subscriba invites you to our CFO Roundtable—a space where financial innovators meet to exchange ideas and redefine tech budgeting for the modern era. Be part of the movement—sign up now."

Five very different ways to say the same thing, but one should stand out as the voice you want your brand to communicate with. Try this exercise, share the drafts with your team, and get feedback from stakeholders to agree on the voice that epitomises your company's DNA. This will serve as the foundation for consistent and impactful communication across all your channels.

Chapter 11
The Role of Authenticity in Modern Storytelling

Here's the hard truth: today's audience can spot inauthenticity faster than you can say "best-in-class solution." It's not enough to craft a story with a perfect arc, compelling characters, and a neatly packaged resolution. If it doesn't feel real, it won't resonate. And if it doesn't resonate, your content is just more noise in an already oversaturated market. Authenticity in storytelling is no longer optional—it's a requirement. So, how do you infuse genuine authenticity into your brand's stories without slipping into the trap of forced relatability?

Why Authenticity Trumps Perfection

You might think your audience wants to hear about your successes, your triumphs, and your innovation. Sure, they do. But if that's all you're offering, you're missing the mark. People don't connect with perfect—they connect with human. They want to see the late nights, the unexpected problems, the almost or the actual failures, and the lessons you learned the hard way. Why? Because they've been there too. And when they see that your brand is willing to share the messy bits, they're far more likely to trust you.

Authenticity in storytelling doesn't mean airing every struggle or overplaying vulnerability for sympathy. It means telling stories that ring true, that show a brand's real experiences, and that don't gloss over the challenges that make the victories meaningful. As we've discussed, perfect hero isn't perfect at all—they stumble, they get back up, and they grow. Your brand should be no different.

How to Make Your Storytelling Authentic

Let Real Voices Speak - Nothing screams authenticity like real voices. Let your customers and team members tell their stories. Showcase real feedback—yes, even the constructive kind—and explain how it inspired change. A customer testimonial like, *"At first, we struggled with the dashboard layout, but Subscriba's team listened to our feedback and improved it within a month,"* is infinitely more relatable than, *"Our clients love our intuitive design."*

Real voices create trust. They remind your audience that there are real people behind your product who care enough to listen and evolve.

Don't Shy Away from Imperfection - Perfect stories are predictable, and predictable stories are forgettable. Think of the KFC "FCK" campaign. They could have issued a standard apology when they ran out of chicken and risked losing credibility. Instead, they leaned into their mistake with humour and humility: a photo of an empty chicken bucket rebranded as "FCK" and a witty, heartfelt message that resonated far beyond their immediate audience. That's how you turn a crisis into a legendary piece of storytelling.

For Subscriba, that might mean talking about the time a beta feature had unexpected hiccups or how the team learned to pivot mid-development. Own your imperfections, and your audience will respect your honesty and root for your brand's comeback.

The Balance Between Authenticity and Professionalism

Being authentic doesn't mean spilling every detail or dropping professionalism. It's about striking a balance—sharing enough to be relatable while maintaining the integrity and expertise your brand stands for. If Subscriba were to share a story about an early setback, it would highlight what was learned and how it improved the product, not just the struggle itself. Authenticity with a purpose is what builds credibility. We've all seen brands try to fake authenticity, and it's cringeworthy. Here's how to avoid it:

Don't Exaggerate Struggles: If a challenge wasn't significant, don't dress it up as a major ordeal. Your audience will see through it.
Avoid Trend-Hopping: If you're only being "authentic" because it's trending, stop. Whilst I was writing the latter chapters of this book there was an almost daily barrage of 'we let GenZ write our advert' type social media posts. Your audience can tell when you're genuine versus when you're just riding the wave.
Stick to Your Values: Authenticity means staying true to what your brand believes in. If a story doesn't align with those values, it's better left untold.

Authentic storytelling makes your audience feel seen and heard. It tells them, *"We get it, because we've been there too."* And when your audience feels that, they're not just passive readers—they're active supporters of your brand. Authentic stories evoke trust, and trust is what converts followers into customers and customers into loyal advocates.

Ask yourself: Is my content real, or is it just polished? If it feels too rehearsed, start revising. Share a story that shows your brand's real journey or a moment where you learned something valuable. If you don't know where to start, pick one authentic story to share in your next piece of content and observe how your audience responds.

Remember, the world doesn't need more perfect stories. It needs stories that feel real, messy, and human—just like the people reading them. Your brand's authenticity isn't just a detail; it's your advantage. Use it.

In this content example we'll look at an email from the product marketing team letting customers know there will be a 2-week delay until the release of version 3.7 due to unforeseen circumstances:

Subject Line: Update on Version 3.7 Release Date
Body: Dear [Customer Name],
We are writing to inform you that the release of Subscriba version 3.7 will be delayed by two weeks due to unforeseen circumstances. We are working diligently to address the situation and ensure that the new version meets our high standards of quality and performance.

We appreciate your patience and understanding. Please know that we are committed to delivering the best possible product to you and will keep you updated on any further developments.

Thank you for your continued support.

Yes, it's clear and informative. It explains the delay but doesn't provide context or insight into the decision-making process, which can make customers feel like they're just being notified, not valued. The value of the communication changes significantly when the company explains *why* there is a delay:

Subject Line: Why Version 3.7 Is Worth the Wait
Body: Hi [Customer Name],
We believe in being transparent, especially when things don't go exactly as planned. The release of Subscriba version 3.7 is going to be delayed by two weeks due to reasons that we didn't

see coming. And while we could gloss over it, that's just not our style.

Here's what happened: during our final round of testing, we discovered an unexpected issue that, if left unaddressed, could impact your experience. Instead of pushing out a release that wasn't up to our standards, we made the tough call to hold back and fix it. Because when it comes to the tools you rely on, we don't believe in compromises.

We know waiting isn't fun, and we genuinely appreciate your patience as we work to get it right. The good news? When version 3.7 does launch, it will be smoother, more efficient, and worth the extra time.

We'll keep you updated along the way, and if you have any questions or just want to know more about what's coming in the release, hit reply—we'd love to chat.

Thank you for being part of the Subscriba community. Your trust means the world to us.

This feels like a decision was made with the customer's best interests at heart. This version of the email creates a sense of transparency and trust, making the brand feel more relatable. It doesn't shy away from admitting that things didn't go as planned, which builds credibility and fosters a stronger connection with the reader. The tone is friendly, empathetic, and conversational, turning a potential disappointment into an opportunity to reinforce the brand's commitment to quality and integrity.

By providing context and using a warm, engaging voice, the email shows that Subscriba values its customers enough to keep them in the loop with honesty. This is how authenticity can transform a simple update into a story that connects and strengthens trust.

Part Two

STORYTELLING IN

SALES & MARKETING

Chapter 12
Turning Your Brand Story into Sales

Storytelling is powerful, but let's not pretend it's just for clicks and warm fuzzies. At the end of the day, you're here to turn stories into sales. The art of storytelling isn't just about connecting with your audience emotionally—it's about guiding them to take action. But how do you transform a compelling brand narrative into a catalyst for conversions?

Why Stories Sell

When done right, stories engage, resonate, and build trust—all essential ingredients for making a sale. Storytelling enhances memory retention and stories help your audience visualise themselves using your product, understand its benefits, and feeling the payoff. The result? A shift from passive interest to active decision-making. In short, stories stick.

But let's not romanticise this too much. The trick isn't just telling a good story; it's telling the *right* story that moves your audience down the funnel. Here's how you do it:

Lead with the Customer's Problem

Start with your customer as the protagonist. People don't want to hear about how great your company is until they know you understand their pain. Illustrate a scenario where your ideal customer finds themselves facing a challenge that your product or service can solve. Make it relatable, and set the stakes high enough that the solution becomes urgent.

Example: "Imagine you're a sales manager halfway through the quarter, staring at a dashboard filled with missed targets. Your team is overwhelmed, juggling multiple tools that don't integrate, and vital leads are slipping through the cracks. The pressure mounts as you realise that unless something changes, hitting your revenue goals will be next to impossible."

This opening draws the reader in by painting a picture that feels familiar and urgent. It sets the stage for your brand to step in as the guide.

Position Your Brand as the Guide

In every great story, the hero needs a mentor—someone who gives them the tools, wisdom, or push they need to succeed. Your brand is that guide. Once you've laid out the challenge, position your product or service as the solution that helps your customer achieve their goals.

Example: "That's where Acme Workflow comes in. Our platform simplifies project management, consolidating all your tasks, timelines, and communications into one intuitive tool. It's like having a personal productivity coach in your corner, ensuring your team hits every deadline without the stress."

Notice how this example doesn't just list features; it focuses on the customer's transformation and how the solution makes their journey easier.

Show, Don't Tell

This golden rule of storytelling applies just as much to brands as it does to novels. Simply stating benefits like "we save time" won't make your audience *feel* the impact. Instead, paint a vivid picture of the transformation your product delivers.

Example: "With Acme Workflow, companies have slashed project delays by 30%. One project manager explained, 'Before Acme, we were constantly firefighting missed deadlines and miscommunications. Now, we're ahead of schedule, and our clients have noticed the difference.'"

Direct quotes and relatable outcomes make the benefits tangible, helping your audience picture their own success story.

Use Micro-Stories to Drive Specific Actions

While overarching brand narratives are important, micro-stories are laser-focused on driving specific actions. These bite-sized tales highlight real-world scenarios that resonate and move your audience toward a decision.

Example: "Take James, an IT specialist for a growing tech firm. He used to spend hours manually tracking compliance deadlines. With Acme Workflow's automated reminders, James cut that time to minutes and avoided a costly missed audit. 'It's a game-changer,' he said, 'for both my sanity and our bottom line.'"

These micro-stories are powerful for social media posts, email campaigns, or case studies. They break down your brand's value into digestible, relatable moments that inspire action while building trust.

Create a Sense of Urgency

A story without urgency is a bedtime tale—pleasant, but with no stakes to inspire action. To convert stories into sales, you need to build urgency into your narrative. This doesn't mean resorting to scare tactics or gimmicks. Instead, highlight why acting now benefits the customer and why waiting could cost them more than just time.

Example: "Quarter-end audits are approaching fast—can your team afford to waste hours searching for missing invoices? Acme Workflow's automated financial reporting streamlines the process, so you can get ahead of the deadline and focus on what really matters."

Urgency sparks action, whether it's signing up for a free trial, scheduling a demo, or making a purchase. When your audience feels the immediate relevance of your solution, they're far more likely to engage.

End with a Clear Call to Action (CTA)

Every story should have a resolution, and in the context of business storytelling, the resolution is what you want your audience to do next. Your CTA should be simple, direct, and compelling.

Example: "Ready to take control of your SaaS landscape and reclaim your budget? Book your free demo today and see how Subscriba can turn your story from chaos to clarity."

Avoid ending your stories with vague suggestions. Make it easy for your audience to understand what step to take next and why it benefits them.

Keep It Real – Authenticity Builds Trust

Nothing kills a sale faster than a story that feels too good to be true. Build trust by being honest about what your product or service can—and can't—do. Share authentic customer stories, including the challenges they faced, and back your narrative with real data. This transparency shows that your brand is grounded in reality, not empty promises.

Example: "When Emma's team started using Acme Workflow, they saw immediate improvements in task tracking but struggled initially with adoption across their global offices. By working closely with our support team, Emma introduced targeted onboarding sessions that brought everyone on board. It wasn't an overnight transformation, but now her team has streamlined communication and exceeded project goals."

This approach demonstrates that your brand understands the complexities of real-world challenges and is committed to supporting customers through the journey, not just the quick wins.

Take Action

Review your current marketing content. Is your brand positioned as the guide, or are you still trying to be the hero? Do your stories end with a clear CTA that drives action? If not, it's time to revise your approach. Try crafting a micro-story for an upcoming email or social post, and watch how your audience responds. Remember, a compelling brand story isn't just told—it's felt, believed, and acted upon.

In this content example we will look an email to a prospect who has met the MQL criteria, but the sales rep has been unable to make contact.

***Subject Line:** Following Up on Your Interest in Subscriba*
***Body:** Hi Rachel,*
I noticed you've engaged with our website, downloaded our ebook, and viewed some of our case study videos. I wanted to reach out and see if you have any questions or need more information about how Subscriba can support your SaaS management needs.

If you'd like to discuss your requirements or schedule a demo, please feel free to reply to this email or book a call at your convenience. We'd love to help you discover how Subscriba can streamline your subscription management process.

Looking forward to hearing from you.

You've probably received (or maybe sent) similar emails. It lists what Rachel has done and invites her to take the next step, but it doesn't evoke curiosity, urgency, or a personal connection to the story. The message reads and feels a lot different when the focus shifts to Rachel's pain points rather than listing her interaction with the brand's website:

> **Subject Line:** *Let's Turn SaaS Management from Chaos to Clarity, Rachel*
> **Body:** *Hi Rachel,*
> *It's no secret that SaaS management can feel like an uphill battle—renewal dates scattered across emails, overlapping tools draining budgets, and unexpected charges creeping in. I've seen firsthand how this silent chaos can slow down even the most efficient teams. And I noticed you've been exploring our content, so you're likely facing some of these challenges too.*
>
> *One of our clients, Faisal, an IT manager, was in a similar spot. His team was constantly reacting to surprise renewals and sifting through spreadsheets that seemed to multiply overnight. When he started using Subscriba, everything changed. Automated reminders, a unified dashboard, and a clear view of costs brought his team from reactive to proactive. They cut redundant expenses and reclaimed valuable hours that went back into driving strategic work.*
>
> *I'd love to hear about the specific challenges your team is navigating and explore how Subscriba can bring you the same clarity and control that made a difference for Faisal. If booking a call has been tricky, no pressure—reply with a time that suits you, or check my calendar here [insert link].*

Looking forward to connecting when the time is right.

This is a simple but relatable customer story that shows transformation and tangible benefits. The email remains personal, recognising Rachel's previous interactions with Subscriba, which adds context and relevance, without listing it out like police evidence. It's been difficult to connect with Rachel, so the CTA is open and non-intrusive, showing willingness to work around her schedule while maintaining a focus on solutions. This helps create an authentic, engaging touchpoint that encourages action without being pushy.

Chapter 13
Crafting a Brand Origin Story That Resonates

Let's get one thing straight: no one wants to hear another bland "we started in a garage" story unless it's true, and even then, it better come with a twist. Your brand's origin story should be more than just a chronological list of events—it should be a tale that grabs your audience by the collar and refuses to let go. Why? Because a strong origin story is the backbone of your brand identity, the foundation of trust, and the springboard for deeper connections with your customers. If your origin story isn't doing this, you're leaving money, engagement, and brand loyalty on the table.

Why an Origin Story Matters

Your brand's origin story isn't just about how you came into existence; it's about why. It's the 'aha' moment that sparked your creation, the obstacle that nearly made you quit, and the belief that kept you going. The best origin stories go beyond the founder's bio and delve into the 'why' that aligns with your audience's 'why.' People don't just buy what you do; they buy why you do it.

A compelling origin story makes your brand relatable, human, and memorable. It's not just a nice touch—it's a necessary one. In a crowded marketplace, your origin story can be the differentiator that sets you apart. It's the emotional hook that turns casual browsers into loyal customers.

The Anatomy of a Great Origin Story

A brand origin story worth telling should have a few key elements:

A Relatable Beginning: Your story should start in a way that your audience can relate to. It doesn't have to be dramatic, but it should be real. Maybe Subscriba started not just with a vision, but with a pain point its founders faced—endless spreadsheets, wasted budgets, and the chaos of managing dozens of SaaS tools.

The Catalyst: What was the turning point that sparked your journey? This could be the moment of frustration, inspiration, or even a failure that made you say, *"There has to be a better way."* Highlighting this moment adds a layer of humanity that data sheets and polished presentations can't touch.

Challenges and Obstacles: Don't just paint a picture of smooth sailing—no one buys it. Real challenges show your audience that you're like them, that you faced uphill battles and kept going. Maybe Subscriba struggled to gain traction in its early days or faced technical hurdles that nearly made the team pivot. Whatever the obstacle, sharing it makes your triumph relatable and inspiring.

The Breakthrough: This is where you turn the corner. It's the moment your audience feels relief and satisfaction, the part where they start rooting for you. It's not just about the success, but what it took to get there—persistence, creativity, teamwork.

The Ongoing Journey: Your story shouldn't end with, *"And we lived happily ever after."* It should show that you're still growing, learning, and evolving. This leaves the door open for your audience to be part of your ongoing journey, fostering a sense of community.

Crafting Your Origin Story

Keep It Real, Keep It Human: Your audience isn't looking for a blockbuster script; they're looking for authenticity. If your brand started because someone threw their laptop across the room in frustration after another SaaS renewal fee hit, say that (with a bit of polish). People relate to raw, human moments more than grand, sweeping statements.

Show, Don't Just Tell: Don't just say, "We struggled with SaaS management." Instead, paint the picture: *"Our team spent countless late nights piecing together renewal dates from spreadsheets and emails, realising we were bleeding money with every missed notification."*

Add Personality: This is your brand's story, so let it reflect your brand's voice. If your brand is witty, don't shy away from injecting humour: *"After our third surprise SaaS bill made us collectively groan, we knew we needed a better solution—or an endless supply of antacid."*

Connect Your Story to Your Audience's Journey: Your origin story isn't just about you; it's about why your journey matters to your audience. Bridge the gap by showing how your experiences align with the pain points, aspirations, or goals of your customers. *"We built Subscriba because we were once in your shoes—managing subscriptions felt like spinning plates, and one was always crashing."*

Common Pitfalls to Avoid

Too Much Self-Congratulation: Remember, this is a story, not an awards acceptance speech. While your accomplishments are important, the focus should be on the journey and lessons learned.

No Emotional Pull: If your story reads like a business plan, it's time to go back to the drawing board. What did it *feel* like during those pivotal moments.

Skipping the Struggles: Don't sanitise your story. Without challenges, your narrative is flat and unrelatable.

A Sample Brand Origin Story Framework

Start: *"We didn't set out to build a SaaS management platform. We just wanted to stop feeling like our budgets were playing hide and seek."*

The Catalyst: *"After our finance lead missed a major renewal that cost us thousands, we knew something had to change."*

Challenges: *"We looked for an out-of-the-box solution on the market, but couldn't find one."*

Breakthrough: *"We asked others how they managed their subscriptions and realised they were struggling too. Then, a late-night brainstorming session led to a 'what if' moment. What if we could create a tool that made SaaS management as intuitive as checking your email?"*

The Journey Continues: *"Today, Subscriba is trusted by companies worldwide, but we're still learning and evolving. Our next chapter? Ensuring no CFO has to guess where their budget is going."*

Take Action

Look at your current 'About Us' section or brand origin story. Does it read like a lifeless résumé, or does it make people want to know more? If it's the former, it's time to rewrite. Draft your brand story using the techniques discussed here. Don't just tell your audience what you do —show them who you are, why you started, and why it matters. Your story isn't just a piece of marketing; it's an invitation for your audience to join your journey.

In the content example let's look at how a founder can convey their origin story as part of a wider investor pitch or keynote speech:

> **Introduction:** *"Good morning, everyone. My name is [Founder's Name], and I'm the founder of Subscriba. I'm excited to be here today to introduce you to our platform. Subscriba is a comprehensive SaaS subscription management tool that helps companies track, manage, and optimise their tech spend.*
>
> **Problem Statement:** *We started Subscriba because we saw that many companies struggle with tracking SaaS subscriptions. Without visibility into renewals, user utilisation, and costs, businesses often face unexpected expenses and inefficient software use.*
>
> **Solution:** *Subscriba consolidates all SaaS data into one dashboard, providing real-time updates, automated renewal reminders, and detailed usage tracking. It helps businesses save money, reduce redundancy, and manage their tech stacks more effectively.*
>
> **Closing:** *I'm proud to say that Subscriba is making a difference for many organisations by simplifying SaaS management and improving financial control. Thank you for your time today, and I look forward to showing you how Subscriba can streamline your SaaS management."*

While it may work for a brief presentation, it's dry and doesn't leave a lasting impression or create a meaningful connection with the audience. What we want to do is bring the story to life by beginning with a relatable moment of frustration:

Introduction: *"Good morning, everyone. I'm [Founder's Name], and today, I want to share the story behind Subscriba —a story that started not in a conference room but with a moment of sheer frustration. Our finance team was buried under an avalanche of spreadsheets, scrambling to find renewal dates and track down elusive invoices. One over-looked subscription renewal fee—one—ended up costing us thousands. That's when it hit me: there had to be a better way.*

The Catalyst: *We weren't alone in this struggle. I spoke with other CFOs and IT managers and heard the same stories of chaotic subscription management—unexpected costs, unused licences, and sleepless nights spent piecing together data. It was clear that managing SaaS should be simple, not stressful.*

The Solution: *That's why we built Subscriba: a platform born out of the need for clarity. Subscriba isn't just a dash-board; it's a game-changer. We designed it to give finance and IT teams real-time insights into their SaaS landscape— renewals, usage, and costs—all at a glance. But more impor-tantly, we built it to take that sense of chaos and replace it with control and confidence.*

A Real Story: *One of our first users, Alex, was managing a fast-growing startup. Before Subscriba, Alex's team was constantly blindsided by surprise renewals and overspending. After using Subscriba, Alex not only cut redundant subscrip-tions but also saved enough to reinvest in his team. 'For the first time,' he told me, 'I'm not reacting—I'm planning.'*

Closing: *So, why does this matter to you? Because whether you're managing a small team or an enterprise, you deserve tools that work for you, not against you. Subscriba is here to simplify your SaaS management so you can focus on what you do best—leading your business to success. Thank you for being here, and I can't wait to show you how Subscriba can change the way you think about SaaS."*

This version paints a vivid picture that the audience can empathise with and sets the stage for why Subscriba exists. By including a real user's experience (Alex's story), the founder adds authenticity and demonstrates the tangible benefits of the platform. The closing not only highlights the product but reinforces the brand's mission to empower users. The tone is personal, engaging, and positions Subscriba as a solution built out of real needs and real stories. It's not just a pitch; it's an invitation to connect and act.

Chapter 14
Storytelling for Product Launches – Captivating Your Audience

When it comes to product launches, you need to step up your storytelling game even further. You're not just telling any story; you're crafting an event and an experience. This isn't just an announcement—it's a call for your audience to stop what they're doing, pay attention, and get excited. So how do you elevate your storytelling for a product launch? Let's go beyond the basics and dive into the subtleties that turn a decent launch into a truly captivating one.

Think back to when we discussed crafting brand origin stories or leveraging customer testimonials to build credibility. Those same principles hold true here, but this time we're blending them into an approach that makes a launch feel less like a pitch and more like an invitation to join something new and transformative. The challenge? You're dealing with a short window where attention is a currency, and the stakes are higher. This is your moment to make an impression, and you don't have time to warm up—every word counts.

To start, consider the hook. You're not just trying to introduce a product; you're opening a story where the audience is instantly invested. It's not enough to say, "We're thrilled to announce..."

because, frankly, who isn't? Your audience isn't waiting to hear how excited you are; they want to know why *they* should be excited. To do this, bring them right into the action. Don't tell them the new feature is here; tell them what life looks like without it. Set the stakes so clearly that your audience can feel the tension even before they know there's a solution. This hook isn't just an attention grabber—it's the first step in making your audience care.

Once you've set the stage, remember what we covered about conflict and resolution. Every compelling product launch story needs an element of struggle, even if it's subtle. It's not just about pointing out a problem; it's about making that problem palpable. Your audience should feel the pinch, the stress, the inefficiency, or the frustration that your product is about to resolve. But here's where you take it deeper: don't make this conflict a monolith. Introduce shades of grey. Maybe the existing solutions are adequate but have a hidden cost—time, effort, or focus. Paint the picture so your audience isn't just nodding along but thinking, *"Yep, that's me."*

When your product enters the story, think of it not as the caped superhero but as the wise guide we discussed in the Hero's Journey. It's not the hero of the story—your audience is. Your product is what equips them to be the hero in their own narrative—their lightsaber if you will. Use your introduction of the product to bridge the emotional gap between frustration and relief. Instead of focusing on what the product does, show what it enables your audience to do. Maybe it's giving them back their evenings, sparing them the awkward team meetings where missed renewals come up, or simply letting them look at a budget without wincing.

But here's where the real nuance of product launch storytelling lies: the transformation. You've set the stakes, introduced the guide (your product), and hinted at the journey. Now, show them what life looks like on the other side. This is more than just listing benefits or tossing out testimonials; it's about using sensory and visual language to make them *feel* the change. Your launch story doesn't end with "It will save you time and money." It ends with, "Your Monday morning looks different now. The spreadsheet chaos is gone, replaced by a single, clear dashboard that lets you start your week with confidence and a second cup of coffee, uninterrupted."

Don't forget the power of personality, as we explored in voice and tone. This is your chance to let your brand's unique character shine through. A touch of wit or a relatable anecdote can go a long way in making your launch feel human and inviting. If your product launch can make your audience chuckle, even better. Because what sticks more: *"Our product tracks renewals,"* or *"Never get that 'oops, we missed it again' renewal email with Subscriba's guard dog-level alert system."*

Now, let's tie it all back. Your product launch should feel like the culmination of every storytelling element we've explored so far. It has a hook, relatable stakes, a clear transformation, and your unique voice layered throughout. This isn't about reinventing the wheel—it's about refining it, so it rolls smoothly and grabs attention. You already know how to tell a story; now, you're honing it to turn a momentary glance into an eager click and an invested customer.

So, as you plan your next product launch, think of it not as a bulletin but as an unfolding scene. Engage them from the start, make them feel the need, present the guide, and leave them imagining their new, improved world. And don't forget to keep it fun. Because if your launch story doesn't make you smile when you're writing it, it's not going to make them smile when they read it, or hear it. Now go out there and launch like you mean it.

Storytelling shouldn't be reserved for sales messages, pitches and website copy, it should also be baked into your internal communications. In this content example let's look at an internal email informing the global team about company's new feature release - Subscriba Alert.

Subject Line: *New Feature Release: Subscriba Alert*
Body: *Hi Team,*
I'm excited to announce the release of our new feature,

Subscriba Alert. This feature notifies users when there are 90 days left on a SaaS contract, providing details such as the contract's cost, the number of licences, and utilisation statistics. This is designed to help users stay ahead of renewals and make informed decisions about their subscriptions.

Please familiarise yourself with Subscriba Alert and be ready to discuss how we can showcase this feature to clients. Feel free to reach out if you have any questions.

This email gets the job done. It announces the feature, explains its primary function, and invites the team to become familiar with it. However, it's missing that spark that makes people stop and really think about why this feature matters. It's a "just the facts" approach that might not engage the team as much as it could. You need your team to understand the transformation that's now possible with this new feature release, so that they, in turn, can tell that story to your customers and prospects.

Subject Line: *Get Ready to Change the Game: Meet Subscriba Alert*
Body: *Hey Team,*
Remember that feeling when a surprise SaaS renewal blind-sides a client and they come to us, frustrated, trying to untangle where the oversight happened? Well, those days are officially numbered. I'm thrilled to introduce Subscriba Alert —our newest feature that's going to redefine how our users manage their SaaS renewals.

Subscriba Alert sends a proactive notification when there are 90 days left on a SaaS contract, complete with the cost, number of licences, and utilisation stats. No more last-minute scrambles or missed opportunities to renegotiate or reallocate unused licences. Just clear, timely insights that empower users to act well before renewal day looms on the horizon.

Think of it as giving our users a head start—like handing them a flashlight just before the power goes out. This is the tool that turns SaaS management from reactive firefighting into a smooth, controlled process. And it's not just a feature; it's another way we're putting our customers back in the driver's seat of their budget.

Take some time to explore Subscriba Alert in action, so when clients come to us with questions (or praise—we'll take that too), you're ready to dive in and show them why this is the upgrade they didn't know they needed but won't want to live without. Let's make sure everyone is up to speed and ready to spread the word.

Have any thoughts or ideas on how we can make this launch even more impactful? My inbox is always open.

This version takes the core information and adds life to it. It opens by painting a relatable scene that the team is all too familiar with— dealing with a client's frustration over missed renewals. This engages the reader from the start and positions Subscriba Alert as the secret weapon that can be wielded by the hero (the customer) to save the day. The feature is described with sensory and visual language, creating a vivid picture of what it means for the user's experience. Phrases like *"like handing them a flashlight just before the power goes out"* add a memorable touch. The email also prompts the team to engage actively and share ideas, making them feel part of the story. It's not just an announcement; it's a rallying cry that makes the team excited and invested in the launch.

Chapter 15
The "Show, Don't Tell" Principle in Marketing

If there's one storytelling rule that's been repeated so often it's practically tattooed on every writer's mind, it's *"Show, don't tell."* And before you sigh and think, *"Yes, yes, I know that one,"* ask yourself this: do your marketing efforts truly show, or do they still just tell? You'd be surprised how often businesses, even the best of them, fall into the trap of listing features and spouting adjectives without illustrating what those features and adjectives *feel like* in action. In marketing, showing doesn't just engage—it captivates, converts, and sticks.

You know the principles, but how do you apply them consistently? How do you resist the urge to drop into *tell* mode when *showing* takes a little more finesse? Let's break it down and make it a natural part of your storytelling arsenal.

"Showing" in marketing means creating a scene so vivid that your audience isn't just reading—they're experiencing. It's the difference between saying *"Our software is user-friendly,"* and describing the sensation of using it: *"With Subscriba, your dashboard greets you like a well-organised workspace—everything in its place, everything within reach, and the chaos of SaaS renewals a distant memory."* The latter invites the audience in, conjures an image, and makes a connection.

The power of showing lies in its ability to make the abstract concrete. *"Our tool saves time"* is telling. But imagine saying, *"With Subscriba's automated notifications, Alex from the finance team can still leave the office at 5 p.m., even during month end—early enough to catch the last of his son's football practice."* That's not just relatable; it's a story. And stories aren't just read—they're felt.

To apply "Show, don't tell" effectively, start by shifting your mindset from explaining benefits to painting benefits. This requires more than a quick fact-drop; it requires an understanding of how your product changes lives, even in small, seemingly mundane ways. Take an example where you might typically say, *"Our clients save money by identifying unused licences."* Now, show it: *"When Sarah, the IT director, saw the Subscriba report that revealed 15 unused licences eating into her budget, she finally exhaled—because in that moment, she knew they were done playing hide-and-seek with their costs."*

It's not about exaggerating or dramatising; it's about finding the stories already present in your product's impact and putting them front and centre. Show how your product slots into the real-world scenarios your audience faces. The more precise the image you can evoke, the more powerful your message will be. People want to see themselves in your marketing, not just hear what it can theoretically do for them.

And let's address an important nuance here: showing doesn't mean bogging down your content with unnecessary detail. It's not about embellishing; it's about choosing the right details. Think of it as curating a gallery. You don't need to show every brushstroke of a painting to make an impact—you need to showcase the details that bring the painting to life.

There's a time and place for telling—when you need to deliver straightforward facts or emphasise a key statistic—but even then, showing can be used as the lead. For instance, you might say, *"With*

Subscriba, teams reclaim an average of 10 hours per month previously lost to manual subscription tracking," and then add, *"That's an extra 10 hours for prioritising strategic projects, team-building, or leaving work on time to beat the rush-hour traffic."*

Ultimately, showing means trusting your audience to make the leap with you. You're handing them the pieces and letting them complete the picture, creating a more interactive and engaging experience. This approach not only makes your message more compelling but fosters a deeper sense of connection. Your audience isn't being told what to feel or think—they're naturally arriving there themselves, guided by the story you're showing.

Now, go back to your current marketing content. Does it make your audience feel like they're in the story, or are they just observing from the outside? Are you showcasing the life-changing (or even day-changing) moments your product creates, or are you just telling people what it does? If it's the latter, it's time to show them what they've been missing. Because in the world of marketing, showing isn't just a principle—it's a superpower.

Chapter 16
Story-Driven Social Media – Content That Engages

Let's be honest: social media is where brand storytelling often goes to die. It's a place filled with uninspired "Happy Friday!" posts, thinly veiled promotions, and content so bland it makes porridge look exciting. Yet, social media has the potential to be a storytelling powerhouse if done right. The challenge is capturing attention in a space designed for infinite scrolls and fleeting interactions. Story-driven content isn't just another option; it's the key to cutting through the noise and making your audience pause, engage, and remember you. So, how do you adapt storytelling principles for social media without sounding like you're trying too hard, or worse, boring people to tears?

First, acknowledge that social media storytelling isn't a direct extension of long-form content. You're not crafting a saga; you're creating micro-narratives—brief moments that still pack a punch. In earlier chapters, we explored the importance of a hook, conflict, and transformation. On social media, these elements need to be condensed but no less potent. Imagine scrolling past, *"We just released a new feature,"* versus pausing to read, *"Ever had a surprise renewal that cost your company £10,000? We did, too, until we built Subscriba's newest feature to stop it from happening again."* Same idea, but one is a bland announcement and the other? A mini-story that intrigues.

The first step is understanding that every post is an invitation to a conversation, not a lecture. And like any good conversation starter, a post should open with something that makes your audience think, react, or feel seen. Social media storytelling means starting in the middle of the action, using relatable language, and then guiding your audience to the takeaway or call to action without them feeling like they're on the receiving end of a sales pitch. This isn't a place for *"Our product saves time."* It's the space for, *"This is how Jane from marketing grew her tech stack by purchasing the most expensive CRM software on the market, without spending additional budget."*

Your voice and tone—discussed in depth in earlier chapters—become even more important here. On social media, there's no time to warm up. Your brand's personality needs to come through in the first few words. If your voice is playful, lean into it. If it's authoritative, start with a confident statement. And don't shy away from a touch of humour or vulnerability when appropriate. A post that reads, *"We missed another renewal, and our budget cried,"* can resonate more than a carefully polished, corporate line.

One of the biggest misconceptions about story-driven social media is that each post must stand alone. But if you've ever gotten hooked on a Twitter thread or followed a brand's multi-part Instagram series, you know that people love a good serialised story. Think of social media not just as a series of one-off posts, but as chapters of an ongoing narrative. This is where you can showcase behind-the-scenes stories, customer journeys, or even the incremental build-up to a product launch. Just remember to keep each post satisfying on its own while teasing what comes next.

There's a nuance to social media storytelling that's often overlooked: it's not just what you say, but how it looks. We've talked about visual and sensory language before, but here, visuals take on a life of their own. Pair your micro-stories with images or videos that don't just accompany your text but add an extra layer to the narrative. A photo of a messy, post-brainstorm whiteboard, a candid shot of your team laughing, or even an animated graphic that highlights a feature can amplify the story you're telling. Social media storytelling thrives on the intersection of text and imagery, where one complements and deepens the other.

And don't forget the golden rule of engagement: it's a two-way street. The story doesn't end when you hit "post." Monitor the comments, respond in a way that furthers the narrative, and engage with users who share their own stories in response. If someone replies to your post with, *"This is exactly what happened to us last quarter,"* don't just like it. Comment back with, *"We hear you—Subscriba's latest feature was built for moments like that."* Keep the story alive by participating in the conversation you started.

Finally, keep in mind that not every story-driven post needs to be about a groundbreaking moment. Everyday moments have power too. The relatable frustration of a late renewal, the joy of simplifying a process, or even a light-hearted behind-the-scenes moment can be just as engaging as big announcements. Remember, social media storytelling isn't about being epic; it's about being real and relevant.

So, before your next post, pause and ask: Does this tell a story or just share an update? Does it invite engagement or just broadcast information? If it's the latter, go back to the drawing board. Social media is where storytelling meets its most impatient audience. If you can win here, you can win anywhere. Let's look how we can announce a new hire via social media:

> ***Text:*** *"We're thrilled to welcome [New Hire's Name] to the Subscriba team as our new Product Manager! [Name] brings a wealth of experience in product development, and we can't wait to see the impact they'll make. Welcome aboard, [Name]!"*
>
> ***Image****: A head and shoulders image of [New Hire's Name]*

This version is concise and professional, clearly announcing the new hire. However, it doesn't go beyond surface-level information. It welcomes the new hire but misses an opportunity to connect their arrival with the values of Subscriba or how they'll bring specific value to the customers and the team.

It changes dramatically when the story goes deeper, linking the new hire's arrival to Subscriba's core values and highlighting the company's commitment to flexibility and remote work:

> **Text:** *"Meet [New Hire's Name], Subscriba's new Product Manager! From the start, we knew [Name] was a perfect fit— not just for their sharp skills in product development, but for their commitment to creating solutions that make life easier for our customers.*
>
> *[Name] joins us remotely from [City/Country], a nod to Subscriba's belief that great work doesn't require a commute, just passion and purpose. With years of experience turning complex ideas into user-friendly tools, [Name] is on a mission to make SaaS management even simpler and smarter.*
>
> *We're excited to see how their fresh ideas and customer-focused approach will shape Subscriba's next chapter, and ultimately empower our users to spend less time managing renewals and more time focusing on what really matters.*
>
> *Welcome to the team, [Name]! Here's to building the future of SaaS management together!"*
>
> **Image**: *A welcoming photo of [New Hire's Name] in their remote workspace, with Subscriba's logo subtly incorporated, such as on a mug or a background banner.*

The storytelling version introduces the new hire as someone with a customer-focused approach, immediately creating a connection between their role and the benefits customers will experience. By painting a picture of the new hire working remotely and focusing on creating user-friendly solutions, the post appeals to both current and potential customers (and potential employees) by reinforcing Subscriba's mission. It feels warm, welcoming, and subtly reminds readers of Subscriba's values and commitment to customer-centric innovation. This approach doesn't just introduce a new team member; it strengthens the brand story and builds trust.

Chapter 17
Using Storytelling in Email Campaigns – From Subject Line to Call-to-Action

Email campaigns have one major thing in common with that daily tsunami of notifications we all get—they're easy to ignore. So, if you're sending out an email campaign that doesn't grab attention, evoke interest, and make readers feel something, you might as well be yelling into the void. Enter storytelling: the unsung hero of email marketing. You know it can elevate your brand content, but in emails, it's not just an enhancement; it's a necessity. Let's explore how to infuse storytelling into every component of your email, from the subject line to the call-to-action (CTA), ensuring that your audience isn't just reading but engaging and acting.

First, the subject line—your email's first (and sometimes only) impression. Think of it as the hook that starts your story. You're not just vying for attention; you're competing against every "Sale Ends Today!" and "Your Invoice is Ready" subject line that's flooding inboxes. To stand out, your subject line needs to tease the narrative within without giving it all away. A line like *"How Alex Cut SaaS Costs and Took Back His Weekends"* isn't just intriguing; it sets up a story and a potential transformation that your readers want to know more about.

Moving into the body of the email, this is where your storytelling needs to shine. Remember, we're not talking about long, winding tales. This is where micro-stories come in handy. Start by grounding your email in a relatable scenario that mirrors your audience's own experiences. It could be the frustration of scrambling to cancel an unexpected auto-renewal or the relief of realising your SaaS expenses are finally under control. The key is to make your reader nod along, thinking, *"Yep, been there."*

But don't stop at just setting the scene. The next step is to guide your audience through a journey—one that subtly weaves in your product as the solution without shouting about it. This is where emails often falter. It's tempting to jump straight from "Here's the problem" to "Buy our solution." Instead, show the impact through the lens of a character or scenario, as we discussed earlier. Instead of saying, *"Subscriba helps you manage your SaaS renewals,"* frame it as, *"With Subscriba's Renewal Guard, Alex didn't just avoid another surprise bill; he finally stopped dreading his email notifications."*

Sensory and visual language plays a role here too. Emails are short, but that doesn't mean they have to be plain. Phrases like *"Imagine opening your dashboard and seeing everything laid out like an organised desk on a Monday morning"* make the reader feel the outcome, not just understand it. If your email reads like a grocery list, you're telling, not showing.

Let's not forget the power of transitions that keep the reader moving seamlessly from the problem to the solution to the payoff. This isn't the time for choppy sentences that break the flow. Every line should naturally lead to the next, creating a sense of anticipation. Think of your email as a short story with an introduction, a climax, and a resolution. *"Frustrated by missed renewals? We were too. But then we built Renewal Guard, and now teams are getting their time— and their budgets—back."*

And now, the crescendo: the CTA. Your call-to-action shouldn't be a flat, one-dimensional demand. If you've told the story well, your audience should be emotionally invested by the time they reach the end. A CTA like *"See how Subscriba can simplify your SaaS management"* works better than *"Try Subscriba now"* because it's a natural extension of the story you just told. It invites readers to continue the journey rather than abruptly asking them to leap.

The takeaway here? Storytelling in email isn't about reinventing the wheel; it's about transforming each part of your email into a cohesive, engaging story that flows. It's about making sure that when your email arrives in an inbox, it doesn't just get opened—it gets read, remembered, and acted on.

So, before you send out your next campaign, ask yourself: Does this subject line intrigue? Does the body tell a story that connects? And does the CTA feel like the natural next step in that story? If not, it's time to go back, tweak, and turn your email into a narrative that engages from start to finish. In this content example, we're going to continue with the topic of email marketing, and look at how to communicate 'bad news' to customers, in this case a 5% price increase:

> **Subject Line:** *Upcoming Price Adjustment Notification*
> **Body:** *Dear [Customer Name],*
> *We are writing to inform you that, effective in 90 days, there will be a 5% increase in our pricing in line with current inflation rates. This adjustment is necessary to continue providing high-quality services and to maintain the standards you expect from Subscriba.*
>
> *We appreciate your understanding and continued support as we make this transition. If you have any questions or would like more information, please do not hesitate to reach out to our support team.*
>
> *Thank you for your attention.*
> **CTA:** *"Contact our support team for any inquiries regarding this change."*

While this email communicates the change clearly and provides a channel for questions, it lacks warmth, engagement, and context. It reads more like an impersonal notification than a conversation, which can leave customers feeling like they're just another number in the system. There's no reassurance of value, no hint of future benefits, and no emotional connection to soften the impact of the news. Let's try a story-driven message that emphasises transparency, customer-centricity, and ongoing commitment:

> *Subject Line:* *Staying Ahead Together – A Note on Our Pricing*
> *Body:* *Hi [Customer Name],*
> *At Subscriba, we've always aimed to provide you with the tools that make SaaS management simpler, more efficient, and ultimately more rewarding. And as you know, we're committed to maintaining transparency and trust every step of the way.*
>
> *Today, I want to share an update with you directly: starting in 90 days, we'll be making a 5% adjustment to our pricing in line with inflation. We've made this decision to ensure we continue offering the highest level of service, supporting the constant improvements and innovative features that help your teams stay ahead.*
>
> *We understand that price adjustments are never ideal, which is why we're giving you a full 90 days' notice to plan and make any necessary adjustments to your budget. And if you're wondering what's coming down the pipeline—get ready. We're rolling out new features that will give you even deeper insights into your SaaS ecosystem, streamline renewals, and continue making your subscription management as smooth as possible.*
>
> *Subscriba has always been about empowering your team to*

spend less time worrying about the details and more time focusing on what you do best. This small adjustment ensures that we can keep delivering on that promise for you now and in the future.

If you have any questions or need to discuss this further, our support team is just an email away.

We're here for you.

Thank you for being a valued member of the Subscriba family. Here's to more growth and fewer surprises (except the good ones).

This email opens with an acknowledgment of the customer's importance and a reminder of Subscriba's mission, setting a positive tone. The price increase is framed not as an isolated event but as a proactive step to continue delivering value. The email uses phrases like *"supporting the constant improvements and innovative features"* to reassure customers that their investment is going toward future benefits. The mention of upcoming features adds a layer of excitement and positions the price increase as part of a larger, customer-focused plan.

The language is warm and direct, creating a sense of partnership rather than detachment. By inviting customers to reach out with questions, the email fosters an open line of communication, reinforcing trust. Overall, the optimised version feels less transactional and more relational, making customers feel included and respected during the change.

Chapter 18
Web Copy That Converts – Transforming Features into Stories

If your web copy reads like a dictionary of product specs and bullet points, it's time for an intervention. You might as well slap on a label that says, *"Here's what we do, but we're too boring to make you care."* No one's getting excited over a list of features unless you show them why it matters. Turning those features into stories transforms your web copy from a wall of text into a living, breathing narrative that compels your audience to stay, engage, and most importantly—convert.

We've covered the basics of storytelling, authenticity, and even micro-narratives in social media. But web copy is its own beast. It sits somewhere between a product pitch and a conversation, aiming to inform while guiding the reader toward action. So how do you make it more than just a placeholder on your website? By embedding stories that illustrate not only what your product does but how it fits into the lives of those using it. Let's dig deeper into how to craft web copy that turns casual visitors into committed customers.

Start with the basics: features tell, but stories show. Anyone can say their software tracks renewals or monitors licence utilisation. But if that's all your web copy does, you're missing the human connection. Instead, show the reader what those features mean in their world. *"Say goodbye to the dreaded last-minute panic when a SaaS renewal slips under the radar. With Subscriba's proactive alerts, your team gets a head start on renegotiations and reallocation, transforming what used to be a scramble into a stress-free, strategic advantage."* Suddenly, "proactive alerts" becomes more than a line on a feature list; it's a solution, a lifesaver, a moment of peace your audience craves.

The secret sauce is anchoring these stories in relatable scenarios. Think back to when we talked about creating relatable characters or positioning your customer as the hero. This approach works beautifully in web copy. Your features should be wrapped in a narrative that frames your user as the protagonist—whether they're a frazzled CFO, an IT director drowning in spreadsheets, or a procurement officer juggling multiple renewals. Your product is their guide, the tool that helps them overcome obstacles, save time, and become the hero of their own workplace story.

But don't just think in terms of problems and solutions. Show transformation. Let your web copy paint a picture of before and after, like any good story arc. Before Subscriba, it's a chaotic scene of missed renewals and budget discrepancies. After Subscriba, it's controlled, predictable, and empowering. Your reader needs to see that journey laid out, not just be told that it exists. Instead of *"Our dashboard provides detailed insights,"* try *"Imagine opening your dashboard and seeing every subscription at a glance, with no more nasty surprises waiting in your inbox. That's what we built Subscriba to deliver."* This isn't just a statement; it's a visual cue that helps your reader step into that moment and feel the relief.

One more thing: web copy isn't the place for a monologue. Invite your reader into the story. Use direct language that speaks to them, like *"you"* and *"your team,"* to make the experience feel personal. Phrases like *"your biggest challenges"* or *"the solution you didn't know you needed"* can resonate much more deeply than third-person descriptions. You're not just explaining what your product does;

you're building a narrative that makes the reader see themselves using it, benefiting from it, and winning because of it.

Web copy is also an opportunity to inject your brand's personality, which, as we've said before, is part of building trust and connection. If your brand voice is witty, let it shine. Don't shy away from saying things like, *"No more chasing invoices like it's an Olympic sport,"* if that aligns with how you communicate. The best web copy doesn't just inform; it entertains and persuades, creating a memorable experience that sticks long after the page is closed.

Now, let's not forget that even the most compelling web copy should lead somewhere. A story without a resolution is just an anecdote. This is where your call-to-action (CTA) comes in, wrapping up the story and guiding the reader to the next step. But keep it consistent with your storytelling. If your narrative has been about taking the stress out of SaaS management, your CTA shouldn't be as dry as *"Request a demo."* Instead, try something like, *"Ready to simplify your SaaS story? Let's get started."* It's a small change but makes a huge difference in maintaining the momentum of the story you've built.

The bottom line? Don't let your features sit like lonely bullet points on your site. Transform them into stories that place your reader in the centre, show them a path from chaos to clarity, and make them feel like the hero they already are—just waiting for the right tool to help them shine. So, look at your web copy and ask: does this tell them what we do, or does it show them why it matters? If it's the former, it's time to turn those features into stories that convert. Let's use this content example to focus on a feature page about Subscriba's utilisation dashboard:

> **Header:** *Utilisation Dashboard – Keep Track of Your Licences*
> **Body:** *Our utilisation dashboard provides an overview of the licences your company has purchased and how many are currently in use. The dashboard also features a health bar that*

indicates the overall utilisation status, helping you make informed decisions about your SaaS subscriptions. With this tool, you can identify underused or unused licences and adjust your spending accordingly.
[Example Image: A screenshot of the utilisation dashboard showing the number of licences bought and used, with the health bar in green and yellow]
***CTA:** Explore the Utilisation Dashboard Today.*

This feature page is clear and gets the point across. It explains what the dashboard does and provides a basic overview of its features. However, it reads like most feature pages—dry and purely informational. It lists benefits but doesn't engage the reader or make them feel any connection to the tool. It lacks a narrative element, leaving the reader with facts but not much motivation to act.

***Header:** Take Control of Your SaaS Licences with Subscriba's Utilisation Dashboard*
***Body:** As CFO, can you easily see how many SaaS subscriptions you're currently paying for? Do you wonder if you're paying for tools that no one's actually using? Now, picture a dashboard that cuts through that chaos, laying out exactly what you've bought, what's being used, and what's gathering digital dust. That's where Subscriba's Utilisation Dashboard comes in.*

With our dashboard, the numbers don't just sit there—they tell you a story. Licences bought versus used are displayed in an intuitive format, and our health bar gives you an instant pulse check on your utilisation status, from "Fully Optimised" to "Time to Reevaluate." No more guesswork, no more waste— just clear, actionable insights that let you decide whether to keep investing or trim the fat.

[Example Video: A quick demo showing the dashboard updating in real-time as users check licences bought/used, with the health bar shifting from yellow to green]

Our Utilisation Dashboard isn't just another tool; it's peace of mind that your budget is being put to work, not wasted. Whether you're rebalancing resources for an upcoming project or cutting costs before the next quarterly review, Subscriba's dashboard empowers your team to act decisively and smartly.
***CTA:** Ready to turn your subscription data into a strategic advantage? Try the Utilisation Dashboard now.*

This version brings the feature to life by opening with a relatable scenario that draws the reader in. It goes beyond telling what the dashboard does and instead shows how it fits into the daily life of someone juggling SaaS expenses. The use of sensory language like *"cuts through that chaos"* and *"pulse check on your utilisation status"* makes the reader feel the benefit rather than just reading about it. The example video complements the copy by visually demonstrating how the dashboard functions, adding an engaging, interactive layer. The CTA isn't a generic *"Explore now"*; it's tailored to continue the narrative, inviting the reader to take the next logical step. This approach helps the reader imagine themselves using the tool, feeling the relief and empowerment it offers.

Chapter 19
Leveraging Storytelling in Video Marketing

If a picture is worth a thousand words, then a video—done right—is worth a thousand stories. But here's the thing: not all videos are created equal. A flashy montage of your product's features set to upbeat music might look great, but will it resonate? Will it stick with your audience after the final frame fades to black? Probably not. That's because great video marketing isn't about visuals alone; it's about storytelling. We're talking about creating videos that don't just show but *tell*—that build an emotional connection, engage viewers, and inspire action.

Video is inherently a storytelling medium, so why do so many brands waste that potential by focusing solely on features or generic corporate jargon? Here's a challenge: take a stroll down memory lane and think about the last video ad that made you feel something. Chances are, it wasn't the one listing product features bullet-point style. It was the one that told a story—a human story, where you saw yourself in the narrative.

Now, let's get practical. The reality is that your audience's attention span isn't just short—it's on life support. Most people will opt for a 20-second video over even the most compellingly written text. And can you blame them? Videos are quick, visual, and memorable. They're bite-sized stories that fit perfectly into the time it takes to wait for a coffee or between meetings. If you're still relying solely on long-form content, you're speaking a language your audience no longer has time to learn.

This isn't just about capturing attention; it's about keeping it long enough to deliver your message. Video content not only engages but also boosts the likelihood of internal sharing. A well-told video story is easy to forward, whether it's to a manager, a procurement team, or a finance department that needs convincing. It becomes your Trojan horse, slipping through the gate to reach stakeholders you didn't even know were watching. The power of a 20-second video that conveys transformation, solution, and excitement is unmatched. Use it wisely.

Start with a protagonist. This could be a relatable customer persona, a team member, or even an animated character if your brand voice leans playful. Whoever it is, they should mirror your audience's challenges and aspirations. For example, imagine a video that opens with Alex, a CFO who's tired of the constant game of *"Where's that renewal alert?"* He's relatable, tired but determined, and your audience recognises themselves in him. They're hooked before you've even mentioned Subscriba.

Next, build the tension. Good stories have conflict, and so should your video. Maybe Alex's team is on the brink of missing another major SaaS renewal that could impact their quarterly budget. The clock is ticking, and the pressure is palpable. But here's where video shines: use pacing, music, and quick cuts to heighten this sense of urgency. Don't just tell your audience what the stakes are; make them *feel* it. The tension pulls them in, makes them invested in the outcome.

Then, enter the guide—your brand. Remember, Subscriba isn't the hero; Alex is. Subscriba is the wise guide that equips Alex with the tools he needs to overcome his challenges. Show Subscriba's dashboard popping up on his screen, displaying those proactive alerts and utilisation stats we talked about earlier. Let your viewers see Alex's moment of realisation, the shift from *"Oh no, not again"* to *"I've got this."* Here's the nuance: don't drown this part in features and benefits. Instead, let the visuals tell the story. The simplicity of the dashboard, the ease with which Alex navigates it, the satisfied nod when he confirms his budget is on track—all of these tell your audience, *"This could be you."*

Now, bring it home with a resolution that goes beyond the screen. Show Alex's team relaxed and laughing over coffee, or giving the go-ahead to a marketing head to purchase more tools, secure in the knowledge costs can be controlled. The shift from tension to relief is what your audience will remember, not just that your product has automated alerts or a sleek interface. They'll recall how it feels to go from overwhelmed to in control—and they'll associate that feeling with your brand.

One of the best parts of video is its capacity for subtle storytelling through detail. The background scenes, the choice of music, even the expression on Alex's face—all contribute to the narrative without needing to be spelled out. It's the ultimate exercise in *"show, don't tell."* Your audience might not remember every feature you highlight, but they'll remember the moment Alex's stress melted away, and they'll think, *"I want that too."*

So, what about even shorter videos or formats like TikTok and Instagram Reels? The same principles apply but on hyperdrive. You don't have the luxury of a slow build, so start in the middle of the action. Grab attention with a relatable hook—*"Ever missed a SaaS renewal and regretted it instantly?"*—and deliver your narrative in rapid, engaging bursts. The pacing may be faster, but the emotional arc should still be there: conflict, guide, transformation.

And let's not forget the importance of consistency in your voice and tone. If your brand is known for being witty, let that come through. Injecting your unique voice keeps the story aligned with your brand's identity, making it memorable.

Finally, don't let your video end on a flat CTA. Make it a natural extension of the story. Instead of a robotic *"Try Subscriba today,"* close with *"Ready to make your team's story stress-free? Let Subscriba be your guide."* It feels authentic, connected, and in line with the journey you just took your audience on.

The bottom line? Your video isn't just a vehicle for information—it's your brand's chance to tell a story that lives rent-free in your audience's mind. So, before you hit "publish" on your next video, ask yourself: Does this show a story that resonates, or is it just another feature reel? In a world where attention is a rare commodity, a well-told story isn't just watched—it's shared, remembered, and acted on.

Chapter 20
Turning Data into Stories – Making Metrics Relatable

Numbers don't lie, but they also don't speak for themselves. Presenting data without context is like serving a gourmet meal without explaining what's on the plate. Sure, it might be impressive, but it leaves your audience guessing and disengaged. Yet, when used well, data can be the backbone of some of the most compelling brand stories. The trick is in translating those cold, hard figures into warm, engaging narratives that your audience can see themselves in. Welcome to the art of turning data into stories.

It's not that people don't care about data; it's that data, on its own, doesn't connect emotionally. And here's a reality that often gets overlooked: even in business, numbers can intimidate people. A sea of percentages and financial figures can create a mental block, leading to disinterest. When you make those numbers relatable, they stop being a source of anxiety and start being a source of inspiration. A percentage point or a revenue figure might interest your finance team, but for most, it needs a story to become memorable. Think back to the last impressive metric you read. Did it make you feel anything? Did it stick with you? Probably not, unless it was framed in a way that resonated beyond the numbers themselves. So, how do you make your metrics relatable, memorable, and worth sharing?

The first step is to shift your perspective on what data represents. Numbers are snapshots of moments—moments of success, struggle, change, and progress. A growth statistic isn't just a metric; it's a testament to the hard work of a team or the trust of your customers. A 20% reduction in costs isn't just savings; it's more budget for growth, innovation, or even keeping the office snack cupboard full (and we all know how vital that is).

Take, for example, the common SaaS metric: user adoption rate. On its own, saying, *"Our user adoption rate increased by 35%,"* might garner a nod of approval, but it's unlikely to do much more than that. Now, let's add a story: *"Three months ago, our product manager, Sarah, faced a challenge: users weren't fully engaging with our new features. Fast forward to today, and thanks to a targeted onboarding initiative, user adoption rates have jumped 35%. Now, teams are spending less time figuring out new tools and more time doing their best work."* Suddenly, that 35% becomes a part of a larger narrative of problem-solving, initiative, and impact.

Metrics become relatable when they're personified—when you attach a name, a face, or a scenario to the numbers. Instead of *"We saved our clients an average of 15 hours a month,"* say, *"For John, the IT manager at a fast-paced startup, those 15 hours meant he could finally catch his breath and focus on proactive projects rather than fire-fighting daily issues."* The data itself is unchanged, but its impact becomes vivid and real.

But what if the data isn't inherently positive? This is where your storytelling muscles really get tested. Let's say your product's churn rate spiked momentarily. Don't just hide it; own it and frame it. *"Last quarter, we saw a 5% increase in churn, and it made us pause. We reached out to understand why, listened to our users, and learned that our renewal process needed an overhaul. We implemented those changes, and the early feedback? Customers are happier, and retention is climbing."* Data-driven stories like these don't just build credibility; they show transparency and a willingness to adapt, which fosters trust.

And then there's the challenge of making repetitive metrics stand out. Let's face it, how many times can you say, *"Our platform has 99.9% uptime,"* before it becomes wallpaper? But tell the story of how that uptime kept a global team seamlessly connected through a major project, despite being scattered across different time zones, and you've got yourself a story that makes that uptime matter. Now, your audience isn't just registering a number—they're visualising what that number looks like in action.

Bringing data into your brand's larger narrative also means showing its real-world implications. A statement like *"Subscriba's clients save an average of 20% on SaaS spend"* is fine, but it's static. Elevate it to, *"For Anna, a CFO at a mid-sized tech firm, that 20% savings meant reallocating funds to invest in the platforms required to create and operate a customer success team."* Suddenly, your data is not just relatable; it's aspirational.

This isn't to say that every metric needs a full-blown backstory, but knowing which data points can be highlighted through story-telling is key. Consider your audience—if you're presenting to a potential client, lead with data that solves a problem they're familiar with. If you're engaging with stakeholders, showcase the numbers that reflect strategic wins, framed in a way that highlights teamwork and forward thinking. Data without a story is just a slide. Data with a story is a narrative that sticks.

And let's not overlook how you present this data visually. A bar chart can tell one story, but a video of a team member explaining how that chart reflects their daily wins? That's a different league. Interactive data that lets users explore stories behind the numbers—such as a case study embedded with client testimonials or a timeline showing growth metrics paired with milestone moments—takes storytelling into an immersive realm. Remember, data storytelling is not about making numbers sound flashy; it's about making them human.

So, the next time you're tasked with turning out a report, a presentation, or a website update, pause and think: Am I presenting these numbers as sterile facts, or am I weaving them into a story worth telling? Because when metrics are made relatable, they don't just inform—they inspire, resonate, and move people to action.

Part Three

DEMONSTRATING

THE IMPACT

Chapter 21

The Customer as the Hero – User-Generated Content Stories

If there's one thing every marketer knows, it's that customers trust other customers more than they trust brands. User-generated content (UGC) isn't just a nice-to-have; it's an untapped reservoir of authentic storytelling that most businesses aren't leveraging to its fullest potential. And here's the best part: UGC isn't just content—it's a story where your customer is the protagonist, their journey is the plot, and your product is the trusty guide that helps them overcome obstacles and reach their goals. In this chapter, we're going deep into how to craft and showcase user-generated content that doesn't just spotlight your customer but elevates them to hero status.

It's tempting to think of UGC as simply customer testimonials or reviews. Sure, those have their place, but when done well, UGC can be so much more than a one-off comment or a tagged photo. It can become the beating heart of your brand's story. The key is to curate and present these stories in a way that resonates with your audience and seamlessly aligns with your brand's overarching narrative. Let's break down how to make that happen.

First, shift your mindset from *"What can our customers say about us?"* to *"What stories are our customers living, and how do we fit into them?"* The difference may seem subtle, but it's critical. Your goal is to uncover the user stories where your product or service plays a supporting but pivotal role. Imagine a video where an influential founder explains how Subscriba's SaaS management tools helped them rein in chaotic spending and funnel those savings back into product development. In that story, Subscriba isn't the hero—it's the catalyst that enables the hero (the founder) to succeed. That's the kind of UGC that resonates because it's genuine, relatable, and inspiring.

But here's where it gets nuanced: finding these stories takes more than a casual scroll through tagged posts. It requires proactive engagement with your community. Reach out to power users who are vocal advocates, ask them open-ended questions about their experiences, and encourage them to share not just what they achieved but the journey it took to get there. It's not enough to say, *"Look at this customer's great results!"* You need to ask, *"What were they dealing with before, and how did our solution change their path?"*

This approach also means leaning into different types of media to tell these stories. A written testimonial is great, but a two-minute user-made video where they share their real-world experience? Even better. Don't underestimate the power of visual storytelling to elevate UGC. Encourage customers to submit video clips, photos, or even short reels that capture their journey. Imagine a series of Instagram Stories from a client's perspective, showing how Subscriba helped them breeze through their quarterly review without the usual last-minute panic. You've now moved from a static review to a dynamic, user-driven narrative that your audience can tap through and feel connected to.

And let's talk about control. Brands often make the mistake of heavily editing or scripting UGC until it loses the authentic voice that makes it so valuable in the first place. Resist this urge. Trust your customers to tell their stories in their own way, even if it's not polished to corporate perfection. The raw, unscripted nature of genuine UGC is precisely what makes it effective.

The most effective UGC doesn't just make the customer the hero; it shows other potential customers that *they* can be heroes too. This emotional connection is the golden ticket to higher engagement, trust, and ultimately, conversions.

Remember, not all UGC needs to be overtly glowing to be impactful. Sometimes, showcasing customer journeys that include challenges and how they overcame them with your help can be even more compelling. Stories that show grit, perseverance, and the "aha!" moment when your product made the difference can make your brand appear more relatable and human. It's okay to feature stories where the customer didn't start out 100% satisfied but ended up finding success and value. This adds layers to your brand's narrative and reinforces that you're not just pushing a perfect product but supporting real people with real challenges.

So how do you showcase these stories effectively? Integrate them throughout your marketing channels, from social media posts to case study spotlights on your website. Turn user testimonials into micro-stories that can be shared as quick LinkedIn updates or featured in email campaigns. Embed short user clips into landing pages to create a richer, more interactive experience. Even your paid ads can benefit from snippets of UGC that show, not just tell, the impact of your product.

Finally, don't forget to recognise and reward the customers who contribute to your brand story. Publicly appreciate them by sharing their stories with your audience, tagging them in posts, and thanking them for being part of your journey. This not only builds goodwill but encourages others to share their own stories, creating a cycle of engagement and authenticity.

In the end, making your customer the hero isn't just about telling the world they used your product—it's about showcasing their journey, complete with highs, lows, and breakthroughs, with your product as the trusty guide that helped them get there. Because when potential customers see themselves in these stories, they don't just see a brand; they see a future they want to be a part of. And that's where the real power of user-generated content lies. For this content example let's look at a script an account manager could use on a call to request a case study for a new customer:

> *Account Manager:* "Hi [Customer Name], this is [Account Manager's Name] from Subscriba. First, I want to thank you for using our platform over the past 90 days. We've been monitoring your progress, and we're thrilled to see the positive impact Subscriba has had on your team.
> I'm calling today to see if you'd be open to contributing to a case study that highlights your experience. We'd love to capture some insights into how Subscriba has helped you manage your SaaS subscriptions more effectively. It would involve answering a few questions about your journey and your key outcomes since using Subscriba.
> Would you be willing to share your experience with us for this case study?"

This script is polite and professional, focusing on collecting a general overview of the customer's experience with Subscriba. While it communicates the request clearly, it lacks depth and specificity. The questions are broad and don't lead the customer toward sharing detailed, narrative-rich insights. The result would likely be a case study that feels flat, more focused on results and features than on the human story behind them.

Now, if we fashion the questions to give us a good chance of getting answers that will fit the storytelling model of case studies, we get something like this:

> *Account Manager:* "Hi [Customer Name], this is [Account Manager's Name] from Subscriba. How are you today? I've been following your team's progress since you started using Subscriba three months ago, and it's been

inspiring to see how you've taken control of your SaaS management.

I'd love to dive a little deeper into your journey so far, particularly the challenges you were facing before Subscriba and the turning points that made a difference. We're putting together a series of user stories to showcase the real impact Subscriba is having, and I immediately thought of your team's story—it's one that I believe other customers will find relatable and empowering.

To create an impactful case study, I'd like to ask a few questions that can guide us through your experience:
What were the biggest pain points or challenges you faced in managing your SaaS subscriptions before using Subscriba?
Can you describe a moment in the past 90 days where Subscriba's features made a noticeable difference for your team? Maybe it was an unexpected win or an avoided problem.

How has your daily workflow changed since implementing Subscriba? Any specific changes that your team has particularly appreciated?
What's one key outcome you've seen so far that you didn't expect but has been a pleasant surprise?
If you could share one piece of advice for other teams considering Subscriba, what would it be?

Your story could inspire other teams navigating similar challenges and show them what's possible. Does this sound like something you'd be open to sharing? Great, let me send these questions over to you and if it's alright with you, let's chat again this time on Thursday?"

This version is conversational, engaging, and positions the customer as the hero of their own story. By framing the request in terms of a *"journey"* and asking specific, open-ended questions, the account manager encourages the customer to share experiences that go beyond surface-level benefits. Questions are tailored to elicit turning points, emotions, and specific changes, which makes it easier to craft a case study that reads like a narrative. This version also subtly reassures the customer that their story has value and could inspire others, making them more likely to participate. The language feels warm, empathetic, and aligns with storytelling principles that engage readers by showing relatable challenges and resolutions.

Chapter 22
Behind-the-Scenes Stories – Humanising Your Brand

Here's the thing about brands: they can feel like faceless entities, corporate robots churning out products, emails, and perfectly curated posts. But nobody bonds with a machine. People connect with people. And while you may be in the business of selling products or services, what you're really doing is asking your audience to trust you. That's where behind-the-scenes stories come in—they're your chance to show that behind the logo and the slick marketing, there's a group of humans who are just as passionate, flawed, and funny as the people you're trying to reach.

A behind-the-scenes story isn't just a photo of your team at the office party with the caption, *"Work hard, play hard!"* No, it's deeper, more nuanced, and, if done well, packed with authenticity. These stories pull back the curtain on your brand and let your audience see what makes it tick. Think of them as the director's cut of your marketing—less polished, more raw, and infinitely more engaging.

First things first, why do behind-the-scenes stories work? Because people are inherently nosy. They love to peek behind the curtain and see what's really going on. It's why blooper reels are often more beloved than the actual movie. Your audience isn't just buying your product; they're buying into your brand's personality, values, and culture. Showcasing the humans behind the business adds layers of relatability and trust that no amount of polished, formal content can match.

Now, don't think of behind-the-scenes content as a spontaneous "post it and hope it sticks" strategy. It should still be storytelling at its core. The best behind-the-scenes stories have a narrative arc: a setup, a moment of insight, and a payoff. Maybe it's the team brainstorming late into the night, fuelled by too much coffee and ambitious ideas, that led to a game-changing feature. Or maybe it's the time your customer support hero, Sam, took a complex problem and solved it with such finesse that even the user's cat clapped. These stories show dedication, challenges, and little wins that make your audience root for you.

And don't underestimate the power of wit and humour here. If your team hit a technical hiccup and spent two hours realising it was just a case of *"turning it off and on again,"* share that. It shows humility and makes your brand human. People love to see that behind the sharp suits and impressive titles, your team isn't immune to classic facepalm moments.

Behind-the-scenes content also gives you the chance to highlight company values in a way that feels authentic. Anyone can say, *"We value innovation,"* but showing your team prototyping, problem-solving, and having those *"aha!"* moments—now that's believable. Maybe your sustainability pledge involves painstaking hours finding eco-friendly suppliers. Share that journey. Let your audience see the sweat, the triumphs, and even the little setbacks that make your brand's promises more than just words.

This type of storytelling is also gold for breaking down barriers and engaging your audience on a personal level. Consider an Instagram Reel that shows snippets of your design team sketching out new ideas, mixed with a clip of someone dramatically saying, *"Back to the drawing board."* Or a LinkedIn post where your CEO reflects on the last time they got hands-on with a project and realised, *"Yep, I still need the team more than they need me."* These moments turn your company into a team of individuals with quirks, challenges, and genuine excitement for what they do.

If you're worried about showcasing moments that seem too mundane or small, don't be. The best behind-the-scenes stories often stem from relatable, everyday experiences. Maybe your office has a ritual of everyone huddling for a five-minute "Wins of the Week" roundup on Fridays. Share that. Let your customers see that you celebrate the big and small wins the same way they do. It's these little windows into your company culture that build a deeper emotional connection.

Remember, behind-the-scenes content should be integrated, not isolated. It shouldn't just live as a one-off post on social media but should weave through your marketing channels, from newsletters to website content. A potential customer scrolling through your "About Us" page should stumble upon not just bios and headshots but stories that give them a sense of the people they'd be working with or buying from.

Think of your brand as a character in its own right. Just like any good character, it needs to be relatable, complete with strengths, flaws, and unique traits. The behind-the-scenes stories are what give your character depth. And when your audience feels like they know your brand well enough to share a laugh or be inspired, that's when you've crossed the threshold from just another business to a brand they care about.

In the end, behind-the-scenes stories are your chance to say, *"Hey, we're real people, just like you."* Because when people see the humanity behind the brand, they don't just remember your product; they remember how you made them feel. And that's the kind of connection that lasts longer than any marketing campaign.

Chapter 23
Collaborative Storytelling – Partnering with Influencers and Ambassadors

Let's face it—brands can tell their own stories all day, but nothing resonates quite like someone else telling your story for you, especially if that someone is an influencer or a trusted ambassador. This is the age of collaborative storytelling, where brands don't just broadcast their message; they share the spotlight and co-create narratives with voices that their audience already trusts. It's time to explore how partnering with influencers and brand ambassadors can amplify your storytelling, infusing it with authenticity, reach, and relatability that goes far beyond what your internal team can achieve alone.

Collaborative storytelling isn't just about handing over the mic; it's about aligning your brand's voice with those of your chosen partners and letting their unique perspective breathe life into your narrative. You can shout from the rooftops about how groundbreaking your product is—but when someone with a loyal following tells their community about how your product changed their workflow, or fixed their biggest business pain, or increased their profitability—it suddenly gains weight. Their story becomes an endorsement wrapped in a relatable experience, giving your brand the kind of credibility that's hard to buy and impossible to fake.

But don't be fooled—collaborative storytelling isn't as simple as recruiting the influencer with the largest following and hoping for the best. It's about choosing the right voices, those whose values, audience, and content style align with yours. If your brand champions sustainability, working with an ambassador known for their eco-friendly lifestyle is a no-brainer. However, choosing an influencer solely based on reach when they're known for high-consumption, trend-chasing content? That's a storytelling misstep waiting to happen.

Now, here's where the magic happens: creating co-branded content that doesn't just regurgitate your existing messaging but adapts and personalises it to fit the voice of your influencer or ambassador. The best collaborations are seamless, where the line between the brand and the storyteller blurs into a single, compelling narrative. This doesn't mean losing control over your message; it means trusting your collaborator to shape it in a way that speaks directly to their audience's hearts and minds.

Take a moment to consider why influencer-driven stories resonate so deeply. It's the personal touch—the moments of candid honesty, humour, or even imperfection that make them relatable. While a brand might highlight features and benefits, an influencer might share the "behind-the-scenes" moments: the late-night realisations, the first reactions, the unexpected challenges. These authentic snippets create a multidimensional story that draws the audience in, making them feel like they're part of the journey, not just passive onlookers.

Ambassadors, particularly long-term partners who are familiar with your brand's mission and products, offer another layer of storytelling potential. Unlike influencers who might share one-off stories, ambassadors become recurring characters in your brand's ongoing narrative. Their experiences and testimonials can shape the perception of your brand over time, building a cohesive story that evolves and deepens with each touchpoint.

But, like any good story, there are potential pitfalls. Collaborative storytelling only works when there's mutual trust, clear communication, and a shared understanding of the brand's core values. Fail to establish these, and you risk ending up with content that feels forced, disjointed, or worse—inauthentic. The audience can sniff out a disingenuous story from miles away, and one misaligned collaboration can dent your credibility faster than a poorly timed post on X.

So, how do you ensure your collaborative storytelling sings? Start by recognising who the influencers or evangelists are within your industry. The cowbells, the early-adopters and the customers who over-share publicly, and start to build genuine relationships with them. Work with them, not just through them. Discuss not only what you hope to achieve but also what excites them about the collaboration. Let them contribute their own ideas—after all, they know their audience better than anyone. When done right, collaborative storytelling is a dance, not a monologue. It's your brand's narrative told with someone else's voice, blending into something more powerful than either could achieve alone.

When your brand's story is amplified through voices your audience already trusts, you're not just telling them why you matter—you're showing them through someone they already relate to. And that's a story that sticks, resonates, and turns casual readers into true believers.

So, get out there and co-create. Your story deserves to be more than a one-man show; it's time to build a cast that makes it unforgettable.

Chapter 24
Storytelling in Employer Branding – Attracting and Retaining Talent

Think about the last time you considered working for a company. Did you jump at a job description just because it had a long list of perks and benefits, or was it the story behind the company that made you pause and think, *I want to be part of this*? The truth is, the best talent isn't drawn to bullet points on a job ad—they're drawn to a narrative that resonates with their values, aspirations, and beliefs. Welcome to the power of storytelling in employer branding.

Employer branding isn't just about how you describe the job; it's about how you position your company's culture, mission, and future. To attract top-tier candidates and keep your current team engaged and motivated, you need more than a polished careers page. You need a story that speaks to who you are, what you stand for, and where you're going. That's where storytelling becomes a game-changer.

Start by considering the story your brand tells prospective employees. Is it one of growth and innovation, a place where ideas are encouraged and nurtured? Or perhaps it's a story of resilience, where challenges have been met head-on and turned into opportunities. The story your brand tells potential hires should make them feel like they're not just joining a company but a journey—one with highs, lows, meaningful milestones and a shared destination.

But it's not just about what's on the surface. Stories that attract talent are those that give a glimpse behind the curtain. It's one thing to say you have a collaborative work environment; it's another to share stories of how that collaboration has led to game-changing projects or personal growth moments for employees. These narratives don't just tell prospective hires what your brand is like; they show it.

Employer branding doesn't stop once the offer letter is signed. Storytelling is just as crucial for retaining talent. Why? Because stories remind your team why they joined in the first place and reinforce their belief that they're part of something bigger. They keep people invested in the brand's mission, even when day-to-day tasks become routine. When employees hear stories of their colleagues' achievements, lessons learned from failures, or moments of collective success, they feel connected to the larger narrative of the company.

One way to harness storytelling for retention is by turning your employees into storytellers. Give them the platform to share their experiences—whether it's a story about overcoming a tough project, finding mentorship within the team, or even a funny moment that highlights the unique culture of your workplace. These stories create a sense of shared experience and belonging that's difficult to replicate with mere facts or corporate slogans.

A strong employer brand story also reflects the company's values and stands on more than just business success. If your brand prides itself on sustainability, diversity, or social impact, those values should be woven into the narrative. Candidates and current employees alike need to see that the company's values aren't just words on a wall but are lived out through real actions and stories.

Storytelling in employer branding is also about evolution. It's about sharing where the company started, the obstacles it has faced, and how it has changed over time. People love to be part of a story that is still being written, especially one where they can see their potential role. If your brand's narrative includes a vision for the future that employees can help shape, that's powerful. It gives them ownership and pride, making them ambassadors of your story, not just characters in it.

But let's be clear: storytelling in employer branding must be authentic. It's no good spinning tales that don't match the reality of the workplace. If a candidate is drawn in by a story about a supportive, innovative culture only to find out the reality is quite different, not only will they leave, but they'll also share their disappointment—taking your carefully constructed brand story down with them. The most compelling stories are honest ones, even if they include moments of imperfection or past missteps. Candidates and employees appreciate transparency and truth more than a fairy tale.

In short, storytelling in employer branding is about creating a narrative that attracts and retains talent by showing them they're part of something meaningful, a place where their contributions aren't just seen but become a chapter in the company's ongoing story. When people can see themselves in your narrative, when they feel that they're stepping into a story worth telling, that's when your employer brand becomes more than a pitch—it becomes a magnet.

So, if you want to stand out in the race for top talent and keep your team invested, take a hard look at the stories you're telling during the recruitment process, onboarding and beyond. Are they just words on a page, or do they have the power to make someone think, *I want to be part of this story*? If it's not the latter, it's time to start rewriting.

Chapter 25

Gamifying Your Brand Story – Creating Interactive Narratives

Picture this: your brand's story, but instead of being told *to* your audience, it's experienced *with* them. This is the power of gamifying your brand story—transforming passive listeners into active participants. In a world where attention is currency and engagement is everything, weaving interactive elements into your storytelling can make the difference between your narrative being a fleeting moment and an unforgettable experience.

Gamification isn't just for tech companies or app developers; it's a strategy that any brand can use to create deeper connections with its audience. It's about adding layers to your storytelling that encourage interaction, challenge your audience to engage, and reward them for being part of your brand's journey. This doesn't mean slapping a game onto your website or adding random points and badges. Effective gamification requires intentionality, tying these elements into your brand's story in a way that feels seamless and compelling.

Think about what makes stories memorable. It's not just the plot; it's the sense of *being in it*, of feeling what the characters feel alongside them, and wondering what comes next. Gamified storytelling takes that one step further. It puts the audience in the driver's seat, making them a co-creator of the narrative. Instead of just reading about a product launch, they might take a quiz that guides them through the decision-making process your team went through. Rather than passively watching a video about your company's values, they might play an interactive scenario where they make choices aligned with those values and see the outcomes.

Why does this work? Because people love to be involved in a story that isn't just happening to them but with them. Gamified story-telling taps into our innate desire for exploration, problem-solving, and accomplishment. When a story is interactive, it doesn't just inform; it becomes an experience that holds attention, fosters loyalty, and builds emotional investment. Your audience isn't just learning about your brand; they're participating in it, and that participation turns into ownership.

One example of this could be a digital journey where your customers make choices that shape how they interact with your product. Imagine a virtual onboarding that allows users to "unlock" levels as they learn more about your features, or a storytelling arc where customers navigate scenarios reflecting real-life challenges solved by your solutions. With every level or choice, they feel rewarded, informed, and more connected to your brand. The story isn't yours alone anymore—it's theirs too.

But interactive narratives don't need to be complex to be effective. Even small gamified elements, like polls or interactive infographics, can enhance how your brand story is experienced. For example, when sharing a case study, turn it into a short "choose your path" scenario, where users can see what could have happened if different strategies were chosen. It's storytelling that not only engages but informs and makes your audience part of the resolution.

The key is to ensure these elements don't feel forced. Gamification works best when it supports the story, not distracts from it. The interactive features should feel like a natural extension of your brand's narrative, enhancing its flow and impact. If your brand is about innovation, create challenges that push users to think outside the box. If your story is about sustainability, build interactive experiences that educate and inspire action toward eco-friendly practices.

There's also the community aspect to consider. Gamified stories can foster collaboration and competition, turning your audience into a community that shares their experiences, compares progress, and motivates each other. A brand story that encourages users to share their own outcomes or compete in leaderboards turns storytelling into a shared, communal event. And when your story becomes the reason a community thrives, your brand moves from a simple presence to a platform.

That said, like any powerful tool, gamification must be used thoughtfully. Interactive storytelling should never sacrifice substance for gimmicks. The most impactful gamified stories are those that keep the essence of storytelling—emotion, relatability, and meaning—at their core. If the interactive element doesn't enhance the story or align with your brand values, it risks coming off as superficial, which can disengage your audience faster than an uninspired press release.

Ultimately, gamifying your brand story is about breathing new life into how people experience your narrative. It shifts storytelling from being a one-way street to an open road where your audience drives alongside you. They learn, laugh, make choices, and feel rewarded for their involvement. And that kind of interaction doesn't just tell your story—it invites your audience to live it.

Chapter 26
Brand Loyalty Through Storytelling – Building Trust and Relevance

Brand loyalty isn't built with discounts, flashy ads, or even perfectly executed products. Those might get you a one-time sale or a positive review, but they won't keep customers coming back for more. What fosters genuine brand loyalty is trust and relevance—two elements that storytelling can deliver better than any bullet-pointed list of benefits ever could.

Trust isn't just given; it's earned, and in a market overflowing with options, relevance is the glue that keeps your audience attached to your brand. But how do you build that trust and relevance through storytelling? Let's dig into how you can use stories to make your brand not just seen but *felt*, creating a connection that goes beyond products and services.

First, understand that brand loyalty is an emotional bond. It's the reason someone will pick your product off the shelf (or click "Add to Cart") even when a cheaper alternative sits right next to it. It's the feeling that *"this brand gets me, and I trust them to deliver."* Storytelling is the most effective way to nurture that feeling because it's inherently human. We're wired to remember stories, not slogans. We're built to connect with narratives, not numbers.

Start by telling stories that showcase your brand's values in action. Anyone can claim they care about sustainability, innovation, or community support. But how does your brand *live* those values? Maybe you've developed a product feature based on customer feedback—share that story. Did your team volunteer to help a local cause, or did you partner with an organisation for a greater good? Show it, don't just state it. A post or video highlighting these stories lets your audience see your values reflected in your actions, which is far more convincing than a static "About Us" page claiming you care.

Next, focus on consistency in your storytelling. Brand loyalty isn't built in a day; it's reinforced through every interaction. Whether it's a customer support email, a social post, or a product launch video, your brand's voice and stories should align with what your audience has come to expect. Think of storytelling as the through-line that connects all your touchpoints. Your audience should feel like they're reading chapters of the same book, not flipping through disconnected articles.

The key here is to make your stories relatable. You're not just telling your brand's story; you're telling your customers' stories back to them. When a customer recognises themselves in the challenges or experiences you share, trust grows. They feel seen, understood, and validated. For example, a testimonial where a small business owner talks about how your product helped them manage their SaaS renewals more efficiently isn't just a nice-to-have; it's a relatable moment for others in their shoes. Your story becomes relevant because it mirrors the audience's reality.

Building relevance means speaking directly to the evolving challenges and aspirations of your audience. Keep your stories current. What's on their minds this quarter? Are they navigating tighter budgets, scaling up, or embracing remote work? Align your brand stories with these contexts. A blog post titled, *"How Subscriba Helped Remote Teams Stay in Sync During Year-End Chaos,"* is more engaging than, *"The Benefits of Our SaaS Management Features."* It's relevant, timely, and framed in a way that the reader can relate to.

Finally, make your stories shareable. When someone reads or watches a story from your brand and feels moved to pass it on to a colleague or post about it on LinkedIn, you're not just building loyalty; you're amplifying it. Sharing stories isn't just about telling your brand's narrative—it's about creating a ripple effect where your audience carries your story forward, becoming your champion and strengthening their relationship with your brand.

The bottom line? Brand loyalty isn't an outcome of flashy ads or generic claims—it's the result of consistent, relatable storytelling that builds trust and shows that you understand your audience's world. When your brand's stories resonate, trust blossoms, relevance solidifies, and loyalty becomes more than just a buzzword—it becomes the heartbeat of your customer relationships.

Chapter 27
Crisis Management – Using Stories to Navigate Challenges

If brands were people, crises would be the messy breakups, the career pivots, and the "I can't believe that just happened" moments. No one is immune to them, and how you navigate a crisis can make or break your brand's reputation. The key? Storytelling. And before you think storytelling in this scenario means spinning a fairy tale that glosses over the ugly bits, let's set the record straight: this isn't about damage control; it's about transparency, empathy, and guiding your audience through your brand's journey with honesty.

When faced with a crisis—whether it's a product recall, a PR disaster, or a sudden service disruption—your instinct might be to stick to a sterile, facts-only approach. And sure, delivering the facts is essential, but if that's all you offer, you're missing an opportunity to humanise your brand and foster trust. Storytelling doesn't mean sugarcoating; it means framing your response in a way that acknowledges the reality of the situation, shows your commitment to resolving it, and leaves your audience feeling heard and reassured.

Start by owning the story. If your brand is going through a crisis, the narrative is going to unfold with or without your input. When you take the lead in telling that story, you have control over how it's perceived. Be the first to address what happened, don't wait to be called out. Start with the facts, but then add context—explain why it happened (as much as you can share), what your team is doing to fix it, and what you're doing to ensure it doesn't happen again. The aim is to take your audience on a journey from confusion or frustration to understanding and even solidarity.

Consider the story of Oatly and their response to backlash over selling a stake to a private equity firm known for investments that some customers felt conflicted with Oatly's sustainable and ethical brand image. The decision sparked criticism and threatened to tarnish Oatly's reputation as an environmentally conscious company. Instead of issuing a sterile press release, Oatly turned the situation into a storytelling opportunity.

They leaned into transparency and shared the story behind their decision. Oatly explained their vision for scaling up to combat larger dairy competitors and outlined how partnering with the firm would help them expand their operations and drive their mission forward. They acknowledged the concerns openly and walked their audience through the dilemma they faced: remain small and limited in impact, or grow with the help of a partner that could accelerate their sustainable agenda.

Sometimes the best storytelling in a crisis is simply empathy. If your product caused a disruption that inconvenienced users, share a story that reflects your understanding of their pain. Maybe an outage affected a small business owner trying to close a deal. Acknowledging stories like these in your response shows you're not just sorry for the inconvenience in an abstract sense—you see the human impact and care about it.

Timing is crucial in crisis storytelling. Your audience shouldn't have to wait days for a response while you're crafting the perfect story. The story doesn't need to be perfect; it needs to be timely and genuine. Begin with a short statement acknowledging the issue, then follow up with more details as you have them. Your initial story should reassure your audience that you're aware of the issue and actively working on it. As you move through the crisis, update the story—share milestones of progress and lessons learned along the way.

When crafting these stories, consider using multiple voices. While the CEO might deliver the initial response to show leadership, updates could come from team leads or even employees who are working on the fix. This approach adds credibility and gives your audience a multi-faceted view of how your brand is handling the crisis. A video from the head of tech explaining how they're tackling a service disruption can build more trust than a nameless email with *"We're working on it."*

Let's not overlook the importance of visual storytelling during a crisis. A simple graphic showing steps your team is taking to resolve an issue or an infographic breaking down what went wrong can make your message more accessible. Visuals can condense complex information into an easy-to-understand format and reinforce that your brand isn't hiding behind jargon. Pairing these visuals with human-focused narratives—like photos or behind-the-scenes clips of the team working hard to resolve the crisis—creates a deeper emotional connection.

Transparency is your greatest ally here. If there was a mistake on your end, own it. Avoid corporate doublespeak like *"We regret any inconvenience"* and try something more direct like *"We missed the mark, and we're taking steps to fix it."* Your audience can tell the difference between a canned apology and an honest one. Trust is built when your story is consistent across all communication channels—from social media updates and press releases to customer emails.

And don't forget to close the loop once the crisis is resolved. The end of the crisis should feel like the conclusion of a story where lessons were learned, improvements were made, and the brand is better for it. A follow-up post or email explaining what changed as a result of the incident can turn a negative experience into a testament to your brand's resilience and commitment to its customers. It's the final act that turns potential detractors into loyal advocates who saw you handle adversity with grace.

In the end, handling a crisis is about more than just putting out fires. It's about showing your audience that your brand is accountable, responsive, and human. The right story at the right time can turn a challenging moment into an opportunity to build trust and strengthen relationships. So, the next time a crisis hits, remember facts tell, but stories reassure and inspire. And when the dust settles, it's the story you told and how you told it that your audience will remember.

Great Examples of Storytelling in Crisis Management

Airbnb – The COVID-19 Response When the COVID-19 pandemic hit, Airbnb faced an unprecedented crisis as global travel came to a halt. The company's CEO, Brian Chesky, addressed the situation with transparent and empathetic storytelling. In an open letter to employees, Chesky announced significant layoffs, but the message stood out for its honesty and humanity. He explained the rationale behind the cuts, acknowledged the pain it would cause, and outlined how Airbnb would support those affected. Chesky's letter shared the company's strategy, the decision-making process, and how they planned to move forward, making employees and the public feel included and respected.

Chipotle – Food Safety Scandals Chipotle faced a significant crisis when outbreaks of E. coli and Norovirus were linked to its restaurants, causing a steep decline in sales and trust. Instead of denying the problem or making vague apologies, Chipotle used story-telling to take ownership and demonstrate their commitment to food safety. CEO Steve Ells appeared on national television to speak directly to customers, explaining what had happened, what they were doing to fix it, and how they would improve safety measures. They also launched a "Commitment to Real Food" campaign that focused on their journey of rethinking and revamping their supply chain, making it clear that they learned from the crisis and were dedicated to earning back trust.

Southwest Airlines – Flight 1380 Emergency In 2018, Southwest Airlines experienced a crisis when an engine failure on Flight 1380 led to the tragic death of a passenger. CEO Gary Kelly's response included a heartfelt video message where he expressed genuine sorrow and empathy for the victims and their families. The airline also provided regular updates and detailed explanations of their safety protocols and plans for future prevention. By addressing the crisis with transparency, empathy, and direct communication, Southwest reinforced their brand's reputation for caring about their customers and safety.

Domino's Pizza – Reputation Rebuilding In 2009, Domino's faced a social media crisis when two employees posted a video showing unsanitary food preparation. Instead of downplaying the situation, Domino's President Patrick Doyle responded with a direct and personal video message. In it, he expressed disappointment, apologised to customers, and outlined the immediate actions the company was taking to prevent similar incidents. This raw, unscripted approach showed accountability and a willingness to make changes, helping to rebuild trust. Domino's also launched a campaign called *"Oh Yes We Did"* that highlighted their commitment to reinventing their product and processes based on customer feedback.

Toyota – Recalls and Safety Concerns During the 2009-2010 recalls due to unintended acceleration issues, Toyota faced a major trust crisis. The company used storytelling in their communication to reassure customers, sharing stories about their engineers working around the clock to identify and solve the issues. They created a series of ads featuring team members talking about their commitment to safety and quality. This approach humanised the brand, showing that Toyota wasn't just a faceless corporation, but a group of people dedicated to doing the right thing.

Nike – Colin Kaepernick Ad While not a traditional crisis, Nike faced backlash when it featured Colin Kaepernick in its 2018 *"Just Do It"* campaign. Kaepernick, known for kneeling during the national anthem to protest racial injustice, was a divisive figure, and many expected the decision to damage Nike's brand. However, Nike leaned into the story, framing it as part of a larger narrative about courage and standing up for what you believe in. The storytelling struck a chord with audiences that valued social justice, reinforcing Nike's brand identity as bold and purpose-driven. While the campaign angered some, it resonated deeply with Nike's core demographic, ultimately boosting sales and brand loyalty.

LEGO – Environmental Commitment When faced with growing criticism over their use of plastics, LEGO didn't dodge the issue. Instead, they told the story of their journey toward sustainability. They shared the steps they were taking, from investing in research for sustainable materials to setting ambitious goals for reducing their carbon footprint. Through video content and social media updates, LEGO made their commitment relatable by featuring employees working on these initiatives and explaining the challenges and milestones in the process. This storytelling approach not only managed the initial criticism but built long-term trust as customers followed their progress.

Patagonia – Environmental Stance Patagonia's *"Don't Buy This Jacket"* campaign wasn't born out of a crisis, but it's a stellar example of using storytelling to pre-emptively address potential criticism and build brand loyalty. The company took a bold stance, acknowledging that consumerism contributes to environmental degradation. They shared stories of how their products were made,

the environmental impact, and their initiatives for repair and recy-
cling. By telling a story that aligned with their values and encouraged
thoughtful purchasing, Patagonia cemented their reputation as an
ethical, customer-centric brand.

Why These Stories Work

In each of these examples, the brands didn't just manage a crisis; they
used storytelling to create transparency, show their values, and
rebuild trust. Whether it was through direct video messages, detailed
blog posts, or campaigns that acknowledged both flaws and commit-
ments, these brands made their audience feel informed, heard, and
part of the journey. That's the power of using storytelling to navigate
challenges—it doesn't just manage the moment; it strengthens the
connection with your audience for the long haul.

Chapter 28
Storytelling Ethics – Navigating Truth and Transparency

It's tempting, isn't it? You've got a story idea that you know could captivate your audience. It has all the right elements—conflict, emotion, a triumphant ending. But there's just one problem: the truth is a little more nuanced. In the world of marketing, where engagement is king, bending the narrative to make it shinier, more inspiring, or more dramatic can seem like a harmless move. But here's the reality check: stories that betray trust might win attention once, but they never build loyalty. And without loyalty, your brand is just noise.

Storytelling ethics aren't a topic that tends to get the spotlight, but they should. In an age where consumers are more informed, more sceptical, and quicker than ever to call out dishonesty, ethical storytelling isn't just good practice; it's essential. People crave stories that resonate, but they also demand honesty. If your brand's narrative is built on half-truths or spin, it's only a matter of time before your audience catches on—and when they do, the damage is real.

So, what does ethical storytelling look like? For starters, it's about striking a balance between telling a story that captivates and staying truthful. This doesn't mean you can't add flair or structure a story for maximum impact. It means ensuring that what you present aligns with the reality of your brand and the experiences of your customers. The moment your story deviates from the truth, you step into the dangerous territory of manipulation. And while an embellished story might get clicks or shares, it's the kind of click-bait engagement that erodes trust.

Take a moment to think about transparency in storytelling. It's not just about sharing the good news; it's about sharing the whole story, even when it includes mistakes, challenges, or outright failures. The brands that have mastered this art know that admitting to struggles or missteps doesn't weaken their story; it humanises it. Consumers see that the brand isn't trying to be perfect; it's striving to be real.

Now, let's talk about where the line is drawn. When does storytelling become manipulation? Picture a brand that tells a tear-jerking story about its charitable initiatives but downplays the fact that these initiatives represent a fraction of its operations. This kind of story might pull at heartstrings in the short term, but it sets the brand up for a credibility crash when the full picture comes to light. True storytelling ethics involve clarity about what your story represents, ensuring that your audience isn't misled.

Ethical storytelling also demands that brands steer clear of exploiting emotions to manipulate their audience. There's a subtle but critical difference between making an emotional connection and exploiting it. The latter might look like a story that leans too heavily on tragedy without offering context or resolution, playing on sympathy rather than genuinely engaging the audience. Your brand's stories should evoke emotion, yes, but they should also respect your audience's intelligence and moral compass.

Consider some brands that have done this well. When Patagonia encourages customers to repair their jackets instead of buying new ones, it's not just a clever story—it's the truth aligned with their mission of sustainability. They tell stories that don't just sound good; they *are* good, and that makes them believable. In contrast, a brand caught stretching the truth—whether by implying a product does more than it does or fabricating endorsements—risks everything. The internet doesn't forget, and neither do your consumers.

So, how do you ensure your storytelling is ethical? Start by vetting every narrative for alignment with reality. If you're telling a customer story, make sure it's accurate and that your customer would recognise themselves in it. Better yet, have them sign off on the content before you publish. If you're sharing a company milestone, acknowledge the journey, including the challenges. Authenticity isn't just about highlighting wins; it's about showing how your brand grows, adapts, and perseveres.

It's also about transparency. If your story involves promises—be it sustainability, inclusivity, or innovation—ensure that you're living up to them. An aspirational story isn't inherently unethical, but it becomes so when the aspiration is passed off as fact. It's one thing to say, "We're working to become carbon neutral by 2030," and another to imply that you already are when that's not the case.

Ethical storytelling is also about context. Sometimes, numbers and statistics are presented in a way that distorts reality. For example, saying "Our sales grew 300%" sounds impressive—until your audience finds out you started with only a handful of units. Storytelling that cherry-picks data without full context risks turning facts into fabrications. Ensure that the stories you tell include enough information to be fair and honest while still being compelling.

Finally, empower your team to practice storytelling ethics as second nature. Just as your brand voice should be consistent across all channels, so should your commitment to truthful, impactful storytelling. Regularly audit your stories, train your team to recognise ethical pitfalls, and create a culture where truth isn't just an option—it's the foundation.

Because here's the thing: audiences can forgive a lot, but being lied to isn't one of them. A story that stretches the truth might get the applause today, but when the curtain falls and the real story is revealed, it's trust that takes the final bow. And once trust is broken, no story, no matter how compelling, can easily win it back.

So, make ethical storytelling your brand's promise. Craft stories that captivate and connect, but let them be rooted in truth, transparency, and respect for your audience's intelligence. Because in the end, the most powerful story you can tell is the one that your customers believe—because it's real.

Chapter 29
Interactive Storytelling in Live Events – Engaging Your Audience in Real-Time

Picture yourself at a live event, sitting among hundreds of people. The lights dim, the speaker steps up, and they start droning through slides packed with bullet points. Within minutes, you're thinking about lunch. Now, imagine a different scenario: the speaker opens with a compelling story, asks the audience to make a choice, and that choice shapes what happens next. A 'Choose Your Own Adventure' audience participation presentation. Suddenly, you're not just a passive observer; you're part of the story. That's the power of interactive storytelling at live events—an experience that engages your audience not just with what you say, but with how you involve them in real time.

Interactive storytelling at live events transforms presentations from monologues into dialogues. It's no longer just a speaker delivering content; it's a shared experience where the audience becomes part of the narrative. This approach works wonders because it taps into a fundamental human desire: the need to feel seen and involved. People don't just want to listen; they want to participate, contribute, and see how their input shapes the outcome.

The beauty of real-time interactive storytelling lies in its ability to adapt and respond. Whether it's a product launch, a keynote presentation, or a workshop, interactive elements keep your audience on their toes. You might use live polls where attendees choose the next topic or share insights on a personal story that changes the course of the event. By involving them, you make the experience unique, memorable, and deeply engaging.

But let's not get carried away; simply sprinkling in some interaction and asking for a show of hands won't magically transform a dull presentation. The key is integrating these elements seamlessly into the story you're telling. For example, in a product demo, don't just explain how your software works—set up a scenario where the audience can guide a live demo through choices that reflect real challenges they face. Each choice leads to different outcomes, making your presentation feel more like an immersive experience than a staged pitch.

Take this scenario: a speaker is presenting a new workflow tool. Instead of showing pre-recorded slides, they invite the audience to choose between two real-world problems—say, managing overlapping tasks or optimising time on projects. Depending on the majority's choice, the speaker demonstrates a tailored solution, weaving in stories of how different clients faced these exact challenges. The audience isn't just learning; they're learning *through* the story they've helped shape. For the storyteller it doesn't matter which variant the audience chooses—the story continues down both paths until the satisfying conclusion.

The impact of interactive storytelling in live events goes beyond entertainment; it deepens retention. When people actively participate in a story, they become emotionally and cognitively invested. Their engagement isn't just surface-level; they remember what they did, why they did it, and what they learned from the experience—and above all they remember the *shared* experience. That's powerful. It turns a one-time presentation into a lasting takeaway, embedding your brand's message in a more meaningful way.

However, like any good story element, interactivity must be

balanced and relevant. Too much interaction, or elements that feel forced, can disrupt the flow and disengage your audience. Think of it as seasoning: enough to enhance the flavour but not so much that it overpowers the dish. Your interactive storytelling should have a clear purpose that serves the larger narrative. Does your audience's input change the story direction, or does it help illustrate key points? If the interaction feels like a gimmick or an afterthought, it will fall flat.

One practical tool for achieving effective interactive storytelling is to use real-time feedback mechanisms—live polling apps, chat functions, or interactive Q&A sessions—that keep the audience engaged while offering insights that inform how the event unfolds. For example, a speaker might pause and pose a question to the audience via a mobile app: "What would you do in this situation?" The responses guide the next segment, making the audience feel like co-creators rather than spectators.

Interactive storytelling also fosters a stronger sense of community. When an audience feels like they've contributed to an event, they bond over the shared experience. Whether it's applauding a popular choice or laughing at a collective mishap, these shared moments turn individual attendees into a unified group, connected by the narrative they've helped shape. And when people feel part of something bigger, they're more likely to talk about it, share it, and remember it.

So, the next time you plan an event, don't just ask, *What do I want to tell them?* Instead, ask, *How can I bring them into the story?* Because when your audience becomes part of the tale, they don't just hear your message—they help shape it, making your brand a story they'll want to tell again and again.

Chapter 30
Measuring the Success of Storytelling – KPIs and Analytics

Storytelling may feel like an art form, but make no mistake—it's one with measurable results. You can't just assume that weaving a compelling narrative into your marketing is working without checking the data. After all, even the most heartfelt brand story needs to translate into actual business outcomes. But how do you measure something as seemingly intangible as storytelling? It's time to put some KPIs and analytics under the spotlight to ensure that your brand's narrative is doing more than just warming hearts; it's driving engagement, loyalty, and revenue.

First, remember that measuring the success of storytelling requires a different lens than standard marketing metrics. Storytelling is both demand generation AND lead generation. It's not as straightforward as tallying up completed online forms or counting clicks, though those certainly have their place. Storytelling is about depth, connection, and long-term value. So, while you'll still look at numbers, you'll need to focus on those that reflect how engaged and emotionally invested your audience is in your brand's narrative.

Let's start with a big one: engagement metrics. These tell you how much your story is resonating with your audience. Are people liking, sharing, and commenting on your social media posts? Is your blog post being passed around like a well-kept secret finally getting its due? Engagement isn't just about clicks; it's about whether your audience feels compelled to interact with your content. High engagement rates mean your story isn't just being seen—it's being felt. Dive into the types of comments and shares to gauge the sentiment. Are people responding emotionally, asking questions, or tagging their colleagues? That's your cue that your story is hitting the mark.

Next, let's talk about time on page and bounce rates. If you're using storytelling on your website, these metrics are vital. When someone lingers on a page, it's a sign that they're not just skimming—they're soaking it in. A story that grabs attention will keep people reading longer and lower your bounce rate. An increase in *average time on page* is a nod that your storytelling approach is working; if your bounce rate drops simultaneously, you've likely succeeded in drawing readers deeper into your narrative.

Scroll depth or below the fold measurement is another unsung hero of storytelling analytics. If your content goes beyond the headline and is structured to tell a story throughout, measuring how far down the page people scroll can reveal where your narrative starts to lose them. If your audience consistently drops off before reaching the end of your story, it might be time to refine your pacing or tighten up your content. Scroll data helps you tweak your story so that it maintains interest all the way through, like a great movie that keeps viewers in their seats until the final credits roll.

Now, onto a metric that puts your audience's commitment to the test: conversion rates. Storytelling isn't just there to make people feel warm and fuzzy; it's there to inspire action. Are people who engage with your story more likely to sign up for your newsletter, download a white paper, or request a demo? Create a funnel analysis that shows the path from initial story engagement to conversion. If storytelling increases conversion rates, it's not just fluff; it's a strategic business asset.

Repeat traffic is a telling metric for long-term engagement. If your storytelling strategy is working, people will come back for more. Check your analytics to see how many users return after engaging with your content. A story that resonates keeps pulling people back in, making your brand a destination rather than a one-off visit. Repeat visitors indicate that your stories are forming part of your audience's ongoing experience with your brand—something that simple ads or product pages rarely achieve.

Social shares and virality metrics ordinarily are the rock stars of storytelling KPIs. If your story gets shared organically, it's a clear sign that it's hitting the right emotional notes. People don't share generic feature lists or bland press releases; they share stories that make them think, laugh, feel inspired, or relate—stories that they think others will enjoy too. Use social media analytics tools to track how far your story spreads and identify which platforms amplify your voice the most effectively.

For more insight into the emotional connection, don't overlook qualitative data like survey feedback or focus group discussions. Directly asking your audience what they felt about a piece of story-telling content can yield surprising insights. You'll understand not just what worked but why it worked, giving you a roadmap for future stories. Even unsolicited feedback from customer emails or direct messages can be a goldmine for understanding the impact of your brand's narrative.

Then, there's brand sentiment analysis. Tools that monitor senti-ment across social media and other digital channels can help you understand how your storytelling is affecting the way people perceive your brand. Are your stories shifting sentiment in a positive direction, or are they being met with a lukewarm response? Regularly track these shifts to adapt and fine-tune your storytelling strategy.

Crucially, is your storytelling impacting customer lifetime value (CLV). If storytelling is doing its job, it's not just boosting immediate conversions but fostering loyalty and repeat business. Track how customers who engage with your storytelling compare to those who don't in terms of retention and repeat purchases. If the CLV of story-engaged customers is higher, you've hit the storytelling jackpot.

Attribution models are also important. Storytelling doesn't always lead directly to a sale, so understanding its role in the buyer's journey is essential. Multi-touch attribution can help identify whether that customer testimonial video or case study nudged someone along the sales funnel, even if it didn't close the deal by itself.

Finally, don't forget to test and iterate. A/B testing isn't just for headlines or button colours; it's for storytelling too. Create different versions of your stories—try one with a customer hero and another with an internal brand story—and see which resonates more. Use the results to refine your approach and make storytelling a continuously evolving part of your marketing DNA.

The bottom line? Storytelling can't be left to intuition alone. It's an art backed by science, where each metric tells a piece of the story about how your audience is connecting with what you're putting out into the world. Because when you measure storytelling not just by how it sounds but by how it performs, you're not just a marketer—you're a strategist who understands that great stories are as powerful in data as they are on the page.

Chapter 31
The Influence of AI and Automation on Storytelling

The era of artificial intelligence and automation has stormed into the world of storytelling, promising streamlined content creation and efficiency that would make any brand's marketing team perk up. AI can churn out copy faster than a team of over-caffeinated writers and generate data-driven insights with a few lines of code. But here's the thing: can an algorithm truly capture the essence of a brand story? Can it evoke empathy, spark curiosity, or inspire action the way a story steeped in human experience can?

Before you put your brand's narrative on autopilot, consider this: storytelling at its core is about plumbing the depths of the human condition. It's about understanding and reflecting the messy, complex emotions that drive people to make decisions, connect, and trust. While AI can mimic these traits, it can't replicate the soul that turns a story from a string of sentences into a moving experience. AI-generated storytelling may be efficient, but efficiency isn't the heart of engagement—authenticity and emotional resonance are.

That's not to say AI and automation don't have their place. When used thoughtfully, they can enhance a brand's storytelling toolkit. AI can help analyse audience preferences, test content variations, and even offer ideas for story structures. It's great for automating parts of the storytelling process that don't need a personal touch—think SEO optimisation, basic customer responses, or quick data summaries. In these areas, AI acts as an assistant, freeing up human storytellers to focus on what they do best: crafting stories that breathe life into a brand.

Yet, here lies the challenge: the temptation to let AI do more. AI can learn from data, identify patterns, and even mimic conversational tones, but it lacks genuine empathy and the nuanced understanding that only comes from lived experience. It can write a competent blog post, but it can't write the post that will make your audience pause, smile, and think, *They really get me*. That's the work of a human storyteller, someone who can see beyond keywords and metrics to what really matters—the story behind the story.

Consider an AI-generated case study. It may include all the right facts, highlight product features, and even wrap things up with a nice conclusion. But without the touch of someone who understands what it's like to face a struggle, celebrate a win, or experience relief, the case study falls flat. It becomes information, not a connection. Brands that rely solely on AI for storytelling risk creating content that feels generic, clinical, and devoid of the quirks and imperfections that make a story memorable.

There's also the issue of trust. Consumers are becoming increasingly savvy and sceptical about content they encounter. They can spot a story that feels manufactured or insincere, and nothing erodes trust faster than a brand that comes across as robotic or detached. Sure, AI can simulate personality, but it can't craft a story that rings true from a place of genuine understanding. To tell a story well, to make it resonate, a brand needs to weave in the subtleties of human emotion—fear, joy, hope, regret—that algorithms simply don't comprehend.

Where AI can be a powerful ally, is when it's used to provide valuable insights and enhance storytelling efforts. For example, using AI tools to sift through customer reviews and social media mentions to uncover common themes and phrases that resonate with your audience. This data can inform human storytellers, giving them the raw material to build stories that speak directly to their audience's experiences and language. AI can handle the heavy lifting of content analysis, but the real storytelling still demands a human touch.

Think of it as a partnership: AI is the diligent researcher who brings you the data, points out trends, and suggests where you might look next. But it's the human storyteller who takes that data and turns it into something that moves people. The AI might suggest, *"Customers like stories about resilience,"* but only a person can tell the tale of a founder's sleepless nights, the gut-wrenching decisions, and the unexpected breakthroughs that ultimately define resilience.

For now, AI can't feel the emotional weight of a story; it can only calculate what might be compelling based on past examples. And while that's impressive, it's not storytelling in the truest sense. The real power of a story lies in its ability to touch something deep within the listener, a spark that says, *I've been there,* or *I get that.* That's why, despite the shiny allure of automation, the most impactful stories will always need human storytellers at the helm, at least for the foreseeable future.

Chapter 32
The Future of Storytelling in Business

Storytelling in business isn't just surviving—it's thriving and evolving at a pace that's impossible to ignore. While the core principles of storytelling remain timeless, how stories are told and consumed is constantly changing. Emerging technologies, new platforms, and shifting audience expectations are reshaping the landscape, and if you want your brand to stay relevant, you need to stay ahead of the curve. But here's a comforting truth: while technology will continue to shape how stories are delivered, the essence of a good story will always resonate, whether it's a ten-second reel or a twenty-minute presentation.

One of the most significant trends shaping the future of story-telling is the rise of immersive technology. Virtual reality (VR) and augmented reality (AR) are no longer just buzzwords—they're tools that brands are using to take storytelling to a new level. Imagine telling the story of a product launch not through a Canva slide deck, but by inviting your customers into a VR experience where they can walk through your product's development journey, see your team in action, and explore the product themselves. AR is also making story-telling more interactive. A print ad can come alive with a quick scan from a smartphone, transforming a static image into a dynamic, engaging story.

Short-form content is another trend that's changed the storytelling game, thanks to platforms like TikTok, Instagram Reels, and YouTube Shorts. The popularity of these platforms has forced brands to condense their narratives into bite-sized stories that grab attention instantly. While this might sound daunting, it's an opportunity. It challenges you to distil your message down to its most impactful elements. The essence of a story that makes someone laugh, think, or share doesn't need a full minute—sometimes, it's just 10 seconds. But, as any good storyteller knows, whether your story is short or long, it still needs a hook, a core message, and an emotional payoff. The format may change, but the fundamentals don't.

That said, long-form storytelling isn't going anywhere. People are still willing to invest time in a compelling narrative, whether it's a podcast series about your brand's origin or a detailed case study that dives into how you solved a major industry problem. The key is knowing your audience and delivering stories in the formats they prefer. A good story works because it's a good story—regardless of whether it's told over two minutes or twenty. Brands that can master both short and long-form storytelling will be the ones that stand out.

Data storytelling itself is evolving, moving beyond simple infographics and static charts to more dynamic, interactive presentations. Using tools that can create interactive dashboards or visual narratives that respond to user input allows brands to tell data-driven stories that are engaging rather than dry. The key here is making the data relatable, turning numbers into narratives. We've touched on this earlier, but the future will see even more sophisticated ways of integrating data with storytelling that feels less like a presentation and more like an experience.

The next frontier in storytelling may very well be personalised, adaptive narratives. Thanks to the growing use of customer data and machine learning, brands can create stories that adapt in real-time to individual user preferences. For example, a customer starts reading a story on your website, and based on their past interactions, the story adjusts to highlight the parts that are most relevant to them. This hyper-personalisation creates a more engaging and unique experience, making your story feel tailored to each member of your audience.

Sustainability and authenticity are also trends that are shaping how stories are being told. Today's consumers, especially GenZ and younger Millennials, are quick to spot inauthentic stories and even quicker to call them out. The future of storytelling will require brands to not just tell stories that sound good but to tell stories that *are* good—transparent, authentic, and aligned with their actions. Brands that fail to back up their storytelling with real-world action will struggle to maintain trust. The story isn't just what you tell; it's what you do, and audiences want to see proof of it in your narrative.

And let's not forget the rise of user-generated content (UGC) as a powerful storytelling tool. Customers are telling their own stories that include your brand, and these stories are more trusted than those created by the brand itself. The future of storytelling will see a blend of brand-driven narratives and customer stories that the brand amplifies and integrates into its overall message. When a customer shares a story about how your product changed their workflow or made their life easier, and you share that story on your platforms, it feels genuine, relatable, and community-driven.

The medium might evolve, but the heart of storytelling remains unchanged: connection. Whether it's a CEO sharing a candid moment in a LinkedIn post, a TikTok highlighting a customer's journey, or a deep dive podcast into your company's milestones, the future of storytelling will always centre around creating a connection. It's about showing that behind every brand is a story worth hearing and that behind every story is a brand worth trusting. The platforms may change, the formats may shift, but the power of a story that resonates is evergreen. The challenge for brands? Staying flexible, authentic, and ready to tell stories in whatever form the future demands.

Chapter 33
Making Storytelling part of your brand DNA

Storytelling isn't just a tactic; it's the lifeblood of a brand that aims to do more than sell—it seeks to resonate, inspire, and stick in the minds of its audience. While many brands dabble in storytelling, few integrate it so deeply that it becomes second nature, woven into every action, decision, and communication. That's the real goal: to make storytelling part of your brand DNA, so that it's not something you occasionally deploy but something that instinctively infuses every touchpoint, from a customer service email to a global marketing campaign.

To start, understand that making storytelling part of your brand DNA means committing to it from the top down. Leadership must champion the value of stories—not just to external audiences but within the organisation. Your employees should know your brand story so well that it becomes their own, shared in meetings, pitches, and even informal conversations. When everyone in the company is aligned on what the brand stands for and can tell that story confidently, you've laid the foundation for storytelling to permeate every level of the business.

Next, train your teams to think like storytellers. This doesn't mean they need to become professional writers, but they should understand the basics of narrative structure: setting the scene, creating tension, and delivering a resolution. Encourage teams to find stories in the everyday operations of your company. Is there a tale behind a feature launch that highlights teamwork or a moment when customer feedback changed your approach? From accounts receivable to customer support, every department has stories that can shine a light on your brand's culture, values, and mission.

Your brand's voice and tone should also reflect your storytelling approach. A company that values storytelling doesn't speak in lifeless, robotic tones. It uses language that invites readers in, sparks curiosity, and evokes emotions. This doesn't mean that every story must be heartwarming or dramatic. It means that even your straightforward product updates or quarterly reports should be presented in a way that connects with the reader. A financial report can highlight the human stories behind the numbers—the innovations that led to those gains or the challenges your team overcame to stay on track.

Making storytelling part of your brand DNA means creating consistency across channels. Your social media, blog posts, press releases, and even internal communications should all carry the same storytelling fingerprint. If a customer reads your latest product release and then sees a tweet from your brand, they should recognise that they're engaging with the same brand voice, one that values narrative and connection. Brands that do this well feel seamless and trustworthy, reinforcing their stories at every turn.

Now, integrate storytelling into customer interactions. Train your sales team to approach pitches as stories, not scripts. Teach customer service to turn even complaint responses into mini-stories that show empathy, resolution, and a commitment to doing better. This is where the magic happens: when storytelling isn't just a marketing strategy but a way of life for your brand.

To make this work long-term, encourage a culture of storytelling. Celebrate the small wins that come from using stories effectively. Share successful storytelling examples in company-wide meetings, whether they're customer stories that resonated or a team member's post that went viral. Recognise and reward employees who contribute stories that exemplify your brand's mission and values. Over time, this creates a self-sustaining environment where stories are not just encouraged but are expected.

Find and use stories everywhere. A customer's offhand comment about how your product made their workday smoother? That's a story. A behind-the-scenes photo of your team pulling together for a launch? Story. The moment when a team member's idea turned a project around? Story. Don't wait for the perfect headline-grabbing narrative to come along; collect and share the stories that reflect who you are, even if they're small. It's in these little moments that your brand's character is built, layer by layer.

Making storytelling part of your brand DNA requires continuous effort, alignment, and reinforcement. But the payoff is immeasurable. When storytelling becomes part of who you are as a brand, your audience doesn't just consume your content—they believe in it, share it, and become part of it.

And the brand lived happily ever after.

The End

Once Upon A Brand Reading List: Elevate Your Storytelling Skills

Building a StoryBrand: Clarify Your Message So Customers Will Listen by Donald Miller (2017, ISBN: 978-0718033323). Offers a proven framework for simplifying your brand's message so customers understand it and take action.

The Catalyst: How to Change Anyone's Mind by Jonah Berger (2020, ISBN: 978-1982108601). Explores the science of persuasion and provides tools to make effective communication that influences change.

Think Again: The Power of Knowing What You Don't Know by Adam Grant (2021, ISBN: 978-1984878106). Encourages readers to challenge their own beliefs and embrace rethinking, essential for authentic storytelling and brand adaptability.

Storyworthy: Engage, Teach, Persuade, and Change Your Life through the Power of Storytelling by Matthew Dicks (2018, ISBN: 978-1608685486). Offers practical advice and exercises for crafting stories that captivate, persuade, and resonate.

Made to Stick: Why Some Ideas Survive and Others Die (Revised and Updated Edition) by Chip Heath and Dan Heath (2020, ISBN: 978-1984883865). Highlights the principles that make stories memorable and impactful, offering strategies to create content that sticks.

You're Not Listening: What You're Missing and Why It Matters by Kate Murphy (2020, ISBN: 978-1250297198). Explores the art of listening and how it enhances storytelling by aligning with the audience's needs and experiences.

The Art of Impossible: A Peak Performance Primer by Steven Kotler (2021, ISBN: 978-0062977533). Provides insights into achieving peak performance, emphasising storytelling elements like overcoming challenges and perseverance.

Cues: Master the Secret Language of Charismatic Communication by Vanessa Van Edwards (2022, ISBN: 978-0593332191). Reveals how to use subtle communication cues to make your brand's storytelling more engaging and charismatic.

Talk Like TED: The 9 Public-Speaking Secrets of the World's Top Minds (Revised and Updated Edition) by Carmine Gallo (2022, ISBN: 978-1250183491). Breaks down the storytelling techniques used by TED speakers to captivate audiences and communicate effectively.

The Power of Regret: How Looking Backward Moves Us Forward by Daniel H. Pink (2022, ISBN: 978-0735210653). Shows how to use stories of past failures and regrets to build relatable, compelling brand narratives.

Hook Point: How to Stand Out in a 3-Second World by Brendan Kane (2020, ISBN: 978-1949001003). Offers strategies for creating impactful content that grabs attention quickly—an essential for storytelling in fast-paced digital spaces.

The Practice: Shipping Creative Work by Seth Godin (2020, ISBN: 978-0593328972). Encourages consistent, meaningful storytelling as part of your brand's creative work, emphasising trust and loyalty.

No Rules Rules: Netflix and the Culture of Reinvention by Reed Hastings and Erin Meyer (2020, ISBN: 978-1984877864). Explores how Netflix's innovative culture and storytelling principles drive success, offering lessons for brand storytelling.

Limitless: Upgrade Your Brain, Learn Anything Faster, and Unlock Your Exceptional Life by Jim Kwik (2020, ISBN: 978-1401958237). Provides strategies for effective communication and mental frameworks that can enhance your storytelling skills.

FOUNDER MODE

Leading with Resilience, Vision, and Purpose

JON SMITH

The Power and Peril of Founder Mode

Founder Mode: Leading with Resilience, Vision, and Purpose celebrates a unique and powerful approach to leadership, one defined by passion, resilience, and an unrelenting focus on innovation. When in founder mode, leaders are deeply embedded in every facet of their business—guiding the vision, fostering direct relationships with customers, and maintaining hands-on control over decisions, especially during the critical early stages. This intense personal investment often drives some of the most successful companies, especially in fast-moving industries. The successes of entrepreneurs like Steve Jobs, who famously guided every major product decision at Apple, or Sara Blakely, who built Spanx by staying directly involved in all aspects of the business, illustrate the immense potential of founder-led companies to revolutionise industries and change the world.

In founder mode, there is a visceral commitment to the company's vision that fuels innovation and grit. Founders bring not just operational oversight, but the kind of creative energy and resourcefulness that transform businesses from ideas into global enterprises. This mode of leadership is what has driven the rapid growth of companies like Shopify, under Tobias Lütke's relentless focus on empowering entrepreneurs, and Glossier, led by Emily Weiss, whose direct connection to her customers fuelled the brand's disruptive success in beauty. The inherent ability to break from traditional rules, embrace risk, and push boundaries is what makes founder mode indispensable in the startup phase, where speed, agility, and direct oversight can make or break a company.

However, the very qualities that make founder mode powerful can, if left unchecked, lead to significant challenges. Founders who remain too deeply entrenched in every decision can stifle their team's growth, inhibit scalability, and risk missing crucial insights that come from external perspectives. Companies that fail to evolve from this mode often find themselves struggling to transition from scrappy startups into sustainable, scalable organisations. When founder mode becomes too rigid, it can foster an echo chamber, where the founder's ideas go unchallenged, leading to potential blind spots, as seen in examples like Theranos, where Elizabeth Holmes' lack of openness to dissenting opinions resulted in catastrophic failures. As businesses grow, leaders must learn to balance the hands-on approach that defines founder mode with strategic delegation and openness to diverse perspectives. The most successful founders evolve their leadership style, bringing in strong executive teams, embracing constructive feedback, and scaling their vision without losing the spark that drove their early success. This book explores the core principles of founder mode—why it matters, how it fuels growth, and the potential risks it carries if not properly balanced.

Ultimately, *Founder Mode* is a celebration of this uniquely entrepreneurial approach to leadership, while acknowledging the delicate balance required to prevent it from becoming a limitation. In a world where innovation is accelerating, founders who master this balance will be the ones who not only build successful businesses but also redefine industries and shape the future.

Chapter 1
Introduction to the Founder Mindset

The concept of the *Founder Mindset* is essential to understanding how successful entrepreneurs navigate the complexities of building and growing a business. Unlike traditional managers, founders operate with a unique blend of vision, intuition, and resilience. This mindset is more than just a style of leadership; it's a way of thinking, decision-making, and problem-solving that directly impacts the trajectory of the business.

At its core, the founder mindset is characterised by three key qualities: visionary thinking, risk tolerance, and relentless execution. These elements define how founders approach challenges, seize opportunities, and navigate the ever-changing business landscape. The intensity and personal investment that founders bring to their work set them apart from managers, who often operate within established frameworks and processes.

Visionary Thinking

Founders tend to think in terms of possibilities rather than limitations. While managers focus on optimising existing systems and processes, founders imagine *what could be.* This visionary thinking often stems from a deep belief in the potential for transformation— whether in an industry, a product, or the world itself. For many founders, the idea of creating something entirely new is what drives them, even when the odds are against them.

For founders, this kind of visionary thinking isn't just an ideal; it becomes a compass that guides the company's strategic decisions. By setting ambitious goals and pursuing innovative ideas, founders inspire their teams and attract early adopters, partners, and investors who believe in the vision. This ability to see beyond what's immediately possible is a hallmark of the founder mindset.

Risk Tolerance

Founders are known for their high tolerance for risk, which stems from their deep personal investment in the success of their ventures. Unlike managers, who often aim to minimise risk through established protocols, founders embrace uncertainty as part of the journey. For them, the possibility of failure is not something to be feared but rather a necessary step toward innovation.

The founder's comfort with risk is deeply tied to their sense of ownership and responsibility. Founders typically have much more at stake than a salaried manager. They have invested not only their financial resources but also their time, reputation, and emotional energy into the success of their company. This leads them to be more willing to take bold risks, because the upside of success aligns directly with their personal goals and vision.

For example, Sara Blakely, the founder of Spanx, risked her savings to start her business when she saw an opportunity to create a product that didn't exist in the market. Despite facing rejections from male executives who didn't understand the concept of shapewear for women, Blakely continued to push forward. Her willingness to take personal and financial risks paid off, as Spanx revolutionised the industry and made her one of the most successful self-made female entrepreneurs.

This mindset is also reflected in how founders approach market conditions. Many successful founders have a contrarian streak; they're willing to take risks on ideas or business models that others dismiss. In doing so, they often redefine industries or create entirely new categories. The ability to take calculated risks, while maintaining the conviction to see them through, is a defining trait of the founder mindset.

Relentless Execution

Perhaps the most visible aspect of the founder mindset is the founder's relentless focus on execution. Vision and risk tolerance are crucial, but without the ability to bring ideas to life, they are merely abstract qualities. Founders often distinguish themselves through their ability to get things done—no matter the obstacles.

This relentless execution is rooted in an intense personal drive and sense of accountability. Founders typically operate with a "do whatever it takes" mentality, particularly in the early stages of a company when resources are limited, and the founder must wear many hats. Whether it's coding the first version of a product, pitching to investors, founder-led sales, or handling customer support, founders are deeply involved in the day-to-day operations of their business.

Relentless execution also manifests in how founders respond to failure. The founder mindset does not treat failure as the end of the road, but rather as an opportunity to iterate and improve. Founders tend to be highly resilient, quickly learning from mistakes and pivoting when necessary to keep their business on course. This ability to adapt and execute despite setbacks is one of the reasons why so many successful founders continue to thrive even after facing early challenges.

One example of relentless execution is Jeff Bezos during the early days of Amazon. Bezos was famously involved in almost every aspect of the business, from packing boxes to answering customer service calls. His dedication to execution laid the groundwork for Amazon's customer-centric approach and operational excellence, which have been critical to its long-term success.

This focus on execution is also what sets founders apart from professional managers. Founders are builders. They create and grow companies through constant action, iteration, and hands-on involvement. The founder mindset is all about making things happen, regardless of the challenges or uncertainties involved.

Founder Mode in the High-Pressure Startup Environment

The startup environment is uniquely suited to the founder mindset because it demands a level of flexibility, adaptability, and creativity that is not typically required in more established companies. Startups operate in a space defined by uncertainty. Whether it's uncertain product-market fit, unproven business models, or volatile market conditions, the founder's ability to thrive in ambiguity sets them apart.

In the early days of a startup, every decision can be critical. There is often no existing playbook to follow, and the margin for error is narrow. In this environment, founders must navigate a combination of limited resources, constant pressure to grow, and the need to pivot quickly based on market feedback. The founder mindset excels here because it embraces this chaos as part of the process.

Startups require leaders who can handle this pressure with a level of personal ownership that goes beyond mere responsibility. Founders are typically involved in every aspect of the business, from product development and customer relations to financing and team building. The need to juggle these roles, often without established processes or systems, and without a full complement of staff, puts extraordinary demands on the founder's time and energy.

This environment is what drives many founders to adopt a "whatever it takes" approach to problem-solving. The founder mindset recognises that in a startup, progress is often made through sheer perseverance, trial and error, and an unyielding focus on the end goal. Unlike in manager mode, where decisions can be slower and more methodical, founders must act quickly to seize opportunities and address challenges as they arise. The high-stakes nature of the startup environment rewards leaders who can make quick decisions, often with limited data, and who can execute.

One prominent example of a founder thriving in this chaotic environment is Reed Hastings, the co-founder of Netflix. In its early days, Netflix was far from the streaming giant we know today. It started as a DVD rental service, and Hastings had to navigate numerous challenges to keep the business afloat. From negotiating with studios to experimenting with subscription models, Hastings demonstrated the adaptability and quick decision-making that define the founder mindset. His ability to pivot Netflix's business model from physical DVDs to online streaming at just the right time highlights how critical it is for founders to stay flexible and open to new possibilities.

The Role of Founders in Shaping Culture and Vision

One of the most critical aspects of the founder mindset in the startup environment is the founder's role in shaping the company's culture and vision. Unlike professional managers who tend to inherit a company's culture and values, founders are tasked with creating these elements from scratch. This is not only a practical necessity but also an opportunity for founders to embed their personal values and beliefs into the company.

Culture is often referred to as the "invisible hand" that guides a company, and the culture a founder creates can influence everything from how teams work together to how they respond to adversity. Founders typically build cultures around their own personality traits, preferences, and working style. In many ways, the startup's culture becomes an extension of the founder's mindset, with qualities like passion, resilience, creativity, and customer obsession often mirrored in the company's ethos.

The founder's vision, meanwhile, acts as a North Star, guiding not just the product or service but also the overall mission of the company. In a startup, this vision is often the key driver of early success. Founders with a clear and compelling vision can inspire their teams to work harder, even in the face of adversity, and can attract investors, partners, and customers who buy into that vision. Unlike professional managers, whose role is often to execute on a pre-defined strategy, founders must create that strategy and continuously communicate it to their teams.

The founder's role in shaping culture and vision can't be overstated. It's often the founder's personal commitment to the vision that keeps the startup moving forward, even when resources are scarce, and success is uncertain. This deep connection to the company's mission is what drives founders to work long hours, make personal sacrifices, and persevere in the face of adversity.

Adaptability: The Key to Surviving Scale

As startups grow and evolve, the challenges founders face also change. While the early days are marked by chaos and rapid iteration, growth introduces a new set of complexities. Founders must adapt to these new challenges without losing the essence of what made their company successful in the first place.

One of the most important qualities of a founder mindset is adaptability. Founders who are too rigid in their thinking or who refuse to delegate responsibilities may struggle as their company scales. In the beginning, it may be possible for the founder to handle multiple roles and make all key decisions, but as the team grows, this approach becomes unsustainable. The founder must learn to build systems and processes that allow for delegation without completely relinquishing control of the company's direction.

Founders often face a critical moment when they must decide how involved they want to remain in the day-to-day operations of the company. Some choose to bring in professional managers to handle the operational aspects of the business while they focus on high-level strategy and vision. Others continue to be deeply involved in the details of their company, maintaining close relationships with employees and customers alike.

The key challenge for founders is knowing when and how to shift gears as the company grows. While staying hands-on is important in the early stages, founders need to develop a leadership style that allows for more structured growth. This doesn't mean abandoning the founder mindset but rather evolving it to meet the needs of a larger organisation. Founders who can adapt their leadership style without losing their vision and passion are often the ones who successfully navigate the transition from startup to scale-up.

Adaptability is not just about scaling leadership but also about responding to changing market conditions. Startups often operate in fast-moving industries, where customer preferences, technology, and competitors can shift quickly. Those who are too rigid in their approach may find themselves left behind, while adaptable founders can turn challenges into opportunities.

Resilience: The Backbone of the Founder Mindset

The journey of building a business is riddled with obstacles, setbacks, and moments of doubt, and it is the founder's ability to push through these challenges that often determines the company's fate. Resilience isn't just about bouncing back from failure; it's about maintaining focus and motivation even when the path forward seems unclear.

In the startup world, failure is often part of the journey. Resilient founders understand that setbacks are temporary and that success requires persistence. This mindset is especially important in industries like technology, where innovation often involves trial and error. Thomas Edison's famous quote, "I have not failed. I've just found 10,000 ways that won't work," encapsulates this resilient mindset. Founders must be willing to fail repeatedly before they find the solution that works.

Creativity: Finding Solutions Where Others See Problems

Creativity is another hallmark trait of successful founders. In many cases, founders create companies not just to fill gaps in the market, but to solve problems in new and innovative ways. Their ability to think outside the box is what allows them to disrupt industries and build products or services that capture the imagination of consumers.

Creative problem-solving is essential in the startup environment, where resources are often limited, and founders must find unconventional solutions to overcome obstacles. This creativity often manifests in the ability to turn challenges into opportunities. Where others might see insurmountable problems, founders see the chance to innovate and differentiate their company.

Creativity in the founder mindset isn't limited to product development. It also extends to how founders build teams, structure organisations, and approach growth. Founders often need to be resourceful and think creatively about how to maximise the impact of limited resources. This can mean finding new ways to motivate employees, securing unconventional partnerships, or identifying non-traditional funding sources. Creative founders are constantly looking for ways to solve problems that others might overlook, and this ingenuity is often what enables their companies to grow and succeed.

Emotional Intelligence: Building Relationships and Leading Teams

While technical skills and business acumen are important, emotional intelligence (EQ) is often the trait that sets great founders apart from the rest. Founders with high EQ are adept at managing their own emotions, as well as understanding and influencing the emotions of others. This is crucial in leadership roles, where founders must motivate teams, navigate conflicts, and build strong relationships with stakeholders.

Emotional intelligence plays a significant role in how founders handle the inevitable stresses of running a company. Founders who are self-aware and able to regulate their emotions are better equipped to deal with the pressures of leadership. They can remain calm and focused in high-pressure situations, which not only helps them make better decisions but also sets a positive example for their team. By managing their own emotional state, founders can lead with confidence and composure, even in times of uncertainty.

In addition to self-management, emotional intelligence is vital in managing relationships. Successful founders are often those who can build strong, trusting relationships with their employees, customers, investors, and partners. This requires a deep understanding of others' motivations, concerns, and aspirations. Founders with high emotional intelligence can inspire loyalty and commitment from their teams because they create an environment where people feel valued and understood.

Persistence: The Drive to Keep Going No Matter What

Starting and growing a company is rarely a linear journey. There are countless setbacks along the way—whether it's a failed product launch, difficulty raising capital, or losing key clients. Founders who succeed are those who keep going despite these setbacks.

Persistence is often linked to passion. Founders who are deeply passionate about their business are more likely to persevere through the tough times because they are personally invested in the success of their venture. This passion fuels their determination and willingness to keep pushing forward, even when the odds are stacked against them.

Persistent founders are often those who can break down large, seemingly insurmountable goals into smaller, more manageable tasks. By focusing on incremental progress and celebrating small wins along the way, they maintain their momentum and motivation. Persistence also means being able to pivot and adapt when things aren't working, rather than giving up entirely.

Managing Stress and Adversity

The founder journey is inherently stressful. The combination of high stakes, uncertainty, and personal responsibility creates a pressure-cooker environment that can take a toll on a founder's mental and physical health. Successful founders are those who learn to manage this stress in a healthy way, ensuring that they can sustain their energy and focus over the long term.

Managing stress doesn't mean avoiding it altogether; it means developing coping strategies that allow founders to maintain clarity and resilience in the face of adversity. This can include everything from time management techniques to mindfulness practices, as well as seeking support from mentors, peers, or mental health professionals.

Arianna Huffington, the founder of The Huffington Post, is a notable advocate for stress management among founders. After collapsing from exhaustion in the early years of her company, Huffington realised that burnout was unsustainable and began advocating for better work-life balance in the entrepreneurial community. Her experience underscores the importance of self-care and stress management for founders who are in it for the long haul.

Chapter 2
Why Founder Mode Matters: The Evolution of Leadership

Leadership in business has undergone significant transformations over the last century. From the rigid hierarchies of early industrial organisations to the flexible, innovation-driven models seen today, the concept of leadership has shifted in response to changing market dynamics, technological advancements, and societal expectations. Central to this evolution is the emergence of what we now call *Founder Mode*—a hands-on, visionary approach to leadership that contrasts sharply with the more traditional *Manager Mode*.

To understand why founder mode matters, it's essential to first explore the historical context of leadership and how it has evolved. Early leadership models were shaped by the needs of large, bureaucratic organisations that prioritised efficiency, standardisation, and control. The rise of the industrial revolution in the late 19th and early 20th centuries gave birth to large corporations where leadership was defined by hierarchy, authority, and a clear division of labour.

Frederick Taylor's theory of *Scientific Management* was one of the most influential models of leadership in the early 20th century. Taylor advocated for breaking down tasks into simple, repetitive motions that could be measured and optimised. Workers were seen as cogs in a larger machine, and the role of leadership was to maximise productivity by strictly controlling the work process. This approach worked well in industries like manufacturing, where efficiency and consistency were critical, but it left little room for innovation or creativity.

As industries grew more complex and globalised in the mid-20th century, leadership theories began to evolve. Peter Drucker, often considered the father of modern management, introduced ideas that expanded the role of leaders beyond mere task management. Drucker emphasised the importance of the *knowledge worker* and the need for leaders to motivate, inspire, and develop their teams. This shift marked the beginning of a more human-centred approach to leadership, where emotional intelligence, collaboration, and adaptability began to play a larger role.

However, even as these ideas gained traction, leadership remained largely hierarchical and management-driven. The role of the CEO or executive team was to set high-level goals and strategies, leaving day-to-day decision-making to middle managers and other department heads. This structure worked well in stable industries where predictability and process optimisation were paramount.

But as the pace of technological change accelerated in the late 20th and early 21st centuries, this approach to leadership began to show its limitations. The rise of the internet, globalisation, and rapid innovation meant that businesses had to be more nimble, adaptable, and creative. It was no longer enough to optimise for efficiency; companies needed to innovate and disrupt to stay ahead. This is where the *founder mindset* began to take centre stage.

The Shift from Managerial Leadership to Founder Leadership

The late 20th century saw the rise of iconic founders like Steve Jobs, Bill Gates, and Richard Branson, who transformed entire industries through their visionary leadership. These founders were not content to simply manage; they were deeply involved in shaping every aspect of their companies, from product design to customer experience. Their leadership style broke away from the traditional manager mode, which focused on delegation, control, and maintaining the status quo.

Founders, in contrast, thrive on *disruption*. They seek to challenge existing norms, create new markets, and solve problems in ways that no one else has imagined. This requires a leadership style that is agile, risk-tolerant, and deeply connected to the core mission of the company. While traditional managers are often focused on maintaining operational efficiency, founders are focused on building something new.

The transition from managerial leadership to founder leadership became especially apparent during the tech boom of the 1990s and early 2000s. Companies like Apple, Microsoft, and Amazon grew rapidly, not because they followed traditional management practices, but because their founders were willing to take risks and innovate. Jeff Bezos, for example, was not content to build a better bookstore; he envisioned Amazon as a platform that would eventually dominate online retail, cloud computing, and media.

Bezos's ability to think beyond the immediate market opportunity and focus on long-term disruption exemplifies the founder mindset. Unlike traditional CEOs, who might prioritise short-term profits or incremental growth, founders like Bezos are willing to make bold, sometimes counterintuitive bets that can reshape entire industries. This visionary thinking is what sets founder mode apart from manager mode and is a key reason why founder-led companies often outperform those led by professional managers.

The Modern Founder: Disruptors and Innovators

As business landscapes continue to evolve in the 21st century, the role of the founder has shifted dramatically once again, cementing them as key disruptors and innovators. Modern founders challenge not just the markets they enter but also the very nature of how businesses are run. Their impact goes beyond mere profitability; they influence societal norms, disrupt traditional industries, and often spark conversations about the future of work, technology, and human behaviour.

Founders as Disruptors

Modern founders are not merely concerned with improving an existing product or service—they are focused on breaking away from conventional systems entirely. These leaders often find success not by iterating on current solutions but by completely rethinking how industries operate. One of the most prominent examples of this is Elon Musk, the founder of The Boring Company and SpaceX. Musk's leadership is a textbook case of founder mode in action—he refuses to accept the limitations of current technology, whether it's in electric vehicles, space travel, or energy storage.

Monzo wasn't the first digital bank, but Tom Blomfield's vision extended far beyond traditional banking services. Blomfield set out to reinvent banking by focusing on transparency, customer experience, and financial empowerment through technology. From real-time spending notifications to no-fee international transactions, Monzo disrupted the financial services industry by offering a product that was deeply user-centric. Monzo didn't just build a bank; it created a community-driven platform that reshaped how people engage with their financesE.

Elon Musk's work at SpaceX is another powerful example of disruption. His goal wasn't simply to make space travel more affordable but to open up the possibility of colonising Mars, a vision that sounds more like science fiction than reality. Yet, his relentless pursuit of this goal has pushed SpaceX to innovate in ways, and at a speed, that traditional aerospace companies could not. Reusable rockets, something that was once thought impossible, are now a key part of SpaceX's business model, enabling significant cost reductions in space missions.

Musk's example illustrates the core of founder mode: a willingness to take extreme risks and to challenge the status quo. This mindset contrasts sharply with traditional managerial leadership, where risk is often minimised in favour of incremental improvement. For modern founders, the focus is not on maintaining the status quo but on creating something entirely new—something that disrupts the current market and forces industries to adapt or become obsolete.

The Airbnb Story: Innovation in Business Models

Another prime example of modern founders as disruptors is Brian Chesky of Airbnb. Like many founders, Chesky saw an opportunity where others saw risk or impossibility. Airbnb started as a simple idea: what if people could rent out their homes to travellers? In the early days, Chesky faced significant scepticism—not only from investors but also from consumers and regulators. The hospitality industry was dominated by large hotel chains, and the idea that people would willingly stay in a stranger's home seemed far-fetched to many.

But Chesky's vision went beyond just short-term rentals; he wanted to build a community of travellers and hosts who could connect on a personal level. His leadership style reflected the founder mode ethos—he was deeply involved in every aspect of the company, from designing the user interface to personally recruiting hosts in the early days. Chesky's hands-on approach, combined with his ability to see the potential for Airbnb to disrupt the hotel industry, was critical to the company's success.

Airbnb is now a global platform, and its impact on the travel industry has been profound. Hotel chains have been forced to adapt their business models to compete with the flexibility and affordability that Airbnb offers. Additionally, cities around the world have had to grapple with new regulations to address the rise of short-term rentals, something that was barely on the radar before Airbnb's disruption.

Chesky's leadership demonstrates another key aspect of founder mode: the ability to adapt and pivot as necessary. In 2020, when the global lockdown devastated the travel industry, Airbnb faced a crisis that could have crippled the company. But instead of retreating, Chesky doubled down on his vision for the future of travel. Airbnb pivoted to focus on long-term stays and rural travel, capitalising on the new demand for remote work and longer stays outside of urban areas. This flexibility and willingness to evolve in the face of external challenges is a hallmark of successful founders.

Balancing Innovation with Operational Efficiency

While founders are known for their visionary thinking and disruptive ideas, scaling these innovations into sustainable business models requires balancing that innovation with operational efficiency. This is where many founders struggle, as the shift from startup to scale-up introduces new challenges. Companies that begin as scrappy, agile startups must eventually introduce more formal structures, processes, and teams to maintain operational efficiency.

However, what sets great founders apart is their ability to maintain their focus on innovation while scaling their operations. Jeff Bezos is a perfect example of a leader who has balanced both. From its humble beginnings as an online bookstore, Bezos grew Amazon into one of the most valuable companies in the world, encompassing everything from cloud computing to entertainment.

Bezos's leadership at Amazon has been marked by a dual focus: on the one hand, relentless innovation, as seen in projects like Amazon Web Services (AWS), Prime, and the company's foray into AI with Alexa; on the other hand, a focus on operational excellence, such as the development of Amazon's world-class supply chain and logistics infrastructure. This combination of long-term visionary thinking, and short-term execution, has made Amazon a dominant player across multiple industries.

For Bezos, maintaining this balance involved creating a culture that embraced experimentation while optimising operations. Amazon famously operates with a "Day 1" philosophy, which encourages employees to think like a startup even as the company has grown to over a million employees. Bezos's ability to infuse the company with an entrepreneurial spirit while maintaining operational efficiency is a model for modern founder leadership.

Redefining Leadership in the 21st Century

Modern founders are not just business leaders—they are redefining what leadership looks like in the 21st century. In traditional corporate environments, leadership has often been synonymous with hierarchy, structure, and delegation. But in the world of startups and disruptive businesses, leadership has become more fluid, collaborative, and visionary.

Founders like Musk, Chesky, and Bezos demonstrate that leadership in the modern era is about more than just managing people or resources—it's about inspiring teams, challenging conventional wisdom, and driving innovation. This new model of leadership prioritises adaptability, customer obsession, and long-term thinking over short-term profits and stability.

Moreover, these founders have reshaped the expectations of what it means to be a leader. In the past, business leaders were often expected to maintain a certain distance from the day-to-day operations of their companies, delegating responsibilities to middle managers and encouraged to enjoy the perks of being the boss, by becoming 'hands off'. In contrast, modern founders are "hands on", often deeply involved in the nitty-gritty of their businesses, from user experience (UX) to customer success. This level of engagement sets a new standard for leadership, where founders are not just figureheads but active participants in every aspect of their companies.

Founder Mode and Its Influence on Business Education and Leadership Programmes

As the influence of founder-led companies continues to grow, it is becoming increasingly clear that the traditional business education model is evolving in response. Business schools, long focused on teaching long-established management theory, operational efficiency, and strategic planning, are starting to integrate more entrepreneurial thinking into their curricula. The rise of *founder mode* as a leadership style has begun to reshape how leadership is taught, with an increasing emphasis on innovation, risk-taking, and agility.

Consider the rise of entrepreneurship programmes in major US business schools such as Stanford's Graduate School of Business and the Massachusetts Institute of Technology's Sloan School of Management. Both institutions have expanded their focus on founder-driven leadership by offering courses that teach students how to think and act like founders. These programmes place a strong emphasis on design thinking, innovation, and disruptive business models. Of course, not all of these graduates will go on to become founders, but they will take their learnings with them to their individual contributor roles, middle management positions, or seats on the executive team. By encouraging students to adopt the mindset of a founder, these schools are preparing future leaders to navigate a rapidly changing business landscape —and begin, or continue, their careers with *founder mode* activated.

Additionally, these programmes are increasingly focused on *experiential learning*, a teaching methodology that mimics the experience of starting a business. Students are given opportunities to develop real-world projects, launch startups, and work through the challenges founders face in their early stages. The ability to experience failure in a controlled environment is particularly important in fostering a founder mindset, as many successful founders attribute their eventual success to learning from early failures.

This shift in education is not just limited to business schools.

Corporate leadership programmes are also adapting to incorporate principles of founder mode. Companies like Google and Slack have launched internal leadership initiatives that encourage employees to think like entrepreneurs, even within large, established organisations. Google's famous 20% time policy, which allows employees to spend one day a week working on passion projects unrelated to their core job, is a direct result of this shift. This policy has led to some of Google's most successful products, including Gmail and Google News.

The long-term impact of these educational shifts is profound. As more leaders are trained to think and act like founders, businesses across industries will likely see a rise in innovation, agility, and resilience. The rigid, process-driven leadership models of the past are being replaced by more dynamic and responsive approaches, shaped by the principles of founder mode.

Founder Mode and Shareholder Expectations

The rise of founder mode has also begun to change the expectations of shareholders and investors. Traditionally, investors prioritised short-term returns, focusing on profitability, cost control, and quarterly earnings. However, as founder-led companies have demonstrated, long-term vision and innovation often deliver greater value over time, even if it means sacrificing short-term profits.

Take the example of Indra Nooyi, the former CEO and Chairperson of PepsiCo, who adopted a founder-like mindset even in a massive, established corporation. Nooyi led a shift towards what she called "Performance with Purpose," integrating long-term sustainability and health-focused initiatives into PepsiCo's core strategy. She moved the company towards healthier snacks and beverages, investing in innovation that would align with shifting consumer preferences and global health trends. Initially, Nooyi's strategy was met with scepticism from shareholders, who were concerned about the impact on short-term profits and consumer confusion. However, her visionary approach ultimately paid off, as PepsiCo experienced steady growth and strengthened its reputation as a forward-thinking company.

This shift towards long-term thinking is becoming more common among investors, particularly in sectors where innovation is critical to survival. Venture capital firms, for example, often prioritise investing in founders with bold, disruptive ideas over more established companies that may offer stable returns but little growth potential. Andreessen Horowitz, one of Silicon Valley's leading venture capital firms, famously looks for founders who "have a vision that changes the world," even if that vision might take years to realise.

Founders who can effectively communicate their long-term vision and build trust with shareholders are more likely to secure the resources needed to execute on their strategies. Whitney Wolfe Herd, the founder of Bumble, exemplifies this ability to balance innovation with investor expectations. Herd's vision for a female-centric dating platform that prioritised safety and respect disrupted the online dating industry. Despite initial pushback from investors who were uncertain about the viability of what appeared to be a niche market, Herd's leadership led Bumble to become one of the most popular dating apps globally. Herd was able to articulate a clear and compelling vision, which not only attracted users but also reassured investors about the company's long-term potential.

The Challenges and Risks of Founder Mode

While founder mode offers many benefits, it is not without its risks. One of the key challenges that founder-led companies face is the transition from a plucky startup to a more structured, scalable enterprise. The very traits that make founders successful—hands-on involvement, risk tolerance, and visionary thinking—can sometimes hinder their ability to manage larger teams or scale operations efficiently.

A notable example of this challenge is WeWork, co-founded by

Adam Neumann. Neumann's leadership was defined by his visionary thinking and bold, ambitious plans to transform office spaces around the world. However, as WeWork scaled, Neumann's inability to transition to a more structured and disciplined leadership style led to significant operational and financial issues. His reluctance to delegate and his erratic decision-making, hallmarks of founder mode, became liabilities as the company expanded. Ultimately, WeWork's IPO collapsed, and Neumann was forced to step down as CEO.

This highlights the importance of evolving leadership as a company grows. Founders must be able to recognise when their leadership style needs to adapt to meet the changing needs of the business. Successful founders often bring in experienced executives or operational leaders to manage day-to-day operations while they focus on the big picture. Evan Spiegel, the founder of Snap Inc., is a good example of a founder who has successfully navigated this transition. While Spiegel remains deeply involved in the vision and strategy of Snapchat, he has surrounded himself with seasoned executives who manage the company's operations, allowing him to maintain focus on innovation.

Additionally, founder-led companies can face governance challenges, particularly when founders hold significant control over voting shares. While founder control can allow for swift decision-making and long-term focus, it can also lead to issues if the founder's interests diverge from those of shareholders. For example, Mark Zuckerberg's control over Facebook (now Meta) has allowed him to maintain a strong grip on the company's direction, but it has also raised concerns about governance and accountability, particularly as the company faces increasing scrutiny over its role in data privacy and misinformation.

Maintaining the Entrepreneurial Spirit as Companies Scale

The final challenge that founder-led companies face is maintaining the entrepreneurial spirit as they scale. Many companies that start with a disruptive, innovative culture struggle to retain that same energy and agility as they grow. The processes and systems that are necessary for scaling can sometimes stifle the creativity and risk-taking that define founder mode.

Maintaining the entrepreneurial spirit requires a conscious effort from founders. They must continually foster a culture of innovation, encourage risk-taking, and ensure that their teams feel empowered to experiment. This can be achieved through organisational structures that prioritise agility, such as small, cross-functional teams, as well as through leadership that rewards creativity and forward thinking.

SCAN THE QR CODE ON THE NEXT PAGE
TO KEEP READING FOUNDER MODE

FOUNDER MODE

LEADING WITH RESILIENCE, VISION & PURPOSE

Keep Reading

About the Author

Jon Smith is an entrepreneur, bestselling author, screenwriter, and business strategist with a track record of founding, scaling, and leading companies to success. Part of the start-up team for Amazon Europe, Jon held leadership positions in major e-commerce and SaaS organisations, including Kitbag.com (acquired by Kleeneze), Book Depository (acquired by Amazon), and Autocab (acquired by Uber).

In addition to his work with large enterprises, Jon founded Toytopia (D2C e-commerce), and Inpress (B2B publisher services). Currently he provides fractional CMO services through Growth-Weaver and is the founder and CEO of Colugo Candles, an eco-luxury e-commerce start-up.

www.jonsmith.net

www.growthweaver.co.uk

www.colugocandles.com

Note from the author

Hi,

Thanks so much for reading *Once Upon A Brand: The Business of Storytelling*.

If you think others would benefit from reading this book, whilst on their own storytelling journey, I would be incredibly grateful if you'd be so kind as to leave a review.

Reviews really help authors for a number of reasons, not least, providing feedback on what readers like, and improving visibility of the book on online retail sites.

Thanks in advance and I wish you well in your storytelling endeavours.

Jon Smith

www.ingramcontent.com/pod-product-compliance
Lightning Source LLC
Chambersburg PA
CBHW071602210326
41597CB00019B/3361